T0208725

THE SWEET
MYSTERY
OF HUMANKIND
and CLIMATE CHANGE

Ed Moore

WESTBOW
P R E S S®
A DIVISION OF THOMAS NELSON
& ZONDERVAN

WestBow Press books may be ordered through
booksellers or by contacting:

WestBow Press
A Division of Thomas Nelson & Zondervan
1663 Liberty Drive
Bloomington, IN 47403
www.westbowpress.com
1 (866) 928-1240

ISBN: 978-1-4908-4727-6 (sc)
ISBN: 978-1-4908-4726-9 (e)

Library of Congress Control Number: 2014914049

Print information available on the last page.

WestBow Press rev. date: 08/27/2014

From the eternal record of humankind: "in the beginning was the Word and the Word was with God, and the Word was God. The same was in the beginning with God. All things were made by him; and without him was not anything made that was made. In him was life; and the life was the light of men. And the light shines in darkness; and the darkness comprehended it not."

Contents

Foreword

Mystery of Life Itself

Humans—what are humans? The answer is that humans are incredible and precious beings that God created in His own image and in His own likeness. Humankind has changed the course of history, the ages, and the very program and purpose of the dark powers of the universe. These dark powers affect the life of each human being on this planet. It is no wonder, then, that they want to cover in mystery all their warfare against God and humankind. God will not allow them to win the war.

Writing to Christian fellowship meetings, the apostle Paul inspiringly wrote in the Word of God, which is also the eternal record of humankind, as follows: "And when I came to you brothers, I did not come with excellent speech of man's wisdom, declaring to you the testimony of God. For I decided not to know anything among you except Jesus Christ, and him having been crucified. And I stood before you in weakness, and fear, and much trembling. And my preaching was not with enticing words of man's wisdom, but in demonstration of the Spirit and of power: that your faith should not stand in the wisdom of men, but in the power of God."

Nevertheless, we speak wisdom among those who are mature. We speak not the wisdom of this world, nor of the princes of this world, who come to nothing; we speak, rather, the wisdom of God in *mysteries,* even the hidden wisdom that God ordained before the world was to our glory. None of the princes of this world knew that hidden wisdom, for had they known it, they would not have crucified the Lord of glory. But, as it is written, no eye has seen, no ear has heard, and no human heart has grasped the things that God has prepared for those who love Him. But God has revealed these things to us by way of His Spirit, for the Spirit searches all things—yes, He searches the deep things of God. For who among us knows the things inside a human being except for the spirit within a human being? So also no one has known the things of God except the Spirit from God. Now we have not received the spirit of the world but the Spirit that is of God, so that we might know the things that are freely given to us of God.

These are the very things I am writing to you about; I write not in the words that I choose from my own wisdom but in the words that the Holy Spirit chooses and teaches. He compares spiritual things with spiritual things (scriptural words with scriptural words), as written in the eternal record. To quote the final authority on this last statement, "These Words that I speak to you, they are Spirit and they are Life."

With all confidence then, we can read and compare all Scripture, knowing we are learning from the Lord, who has all power in heaven and earth! But the natural person does not believe nor receive these teachings of the Spirit of God, because they are foolishness to such a person. Neither can such a person know them, because these truths are spiritually discerned. But a person who is spiritual carefully examines these things judiciously. We who have the mind of Christ now begin to open the mysteries.

1

Time in a Great Mystery

The great mystery of humankind is revealed to us as a function of *time*! Everything we know about humankind is revealed within certain and specified times. We define these as areas of time, as subdivisions of *infinite time*, which is *eternity*. Within each area there are divisions called administrations.

Time Area 1

Time area 1 we refer to as "pre-beginning." Everything we know about ourselves has a beginning and also an end on this earth, when we think about life. However, time *without us* existed *unending* before humankind was created; we call this pre-human time "time area 1." We have an account of great events that took place during that area, given to us in the book of Job. Job lived in ancient times, and his book, inspired of God, is part of the written eternal record of humankind that we call the

Word of God or Holy Bible. This account is now presented from the eternal record:

"Then the Lord answered job out of the whirlwind, and said, who is this who speaks words not based on knowledge of the facts? Buckle up like a man; for I will demand answers of you. Where were you when I conceived the design of the foundations of the earth? Declare it if you have understanding of the truth Who designed the dimensions of it if you know? Or who was able measure it? Where are the foundations of it anchored? Or who laid the Corners of it? When the *Shining* Princes sang together; and *all the sons of God shouted with joy*?" Now we must refer to time again, because God is speaking *of time before humankind was created* and *not* time area 2, when Job's ancestor, Adam, was created. This becomes a great mystery, and we have the answer in the eternal record if we examine it carefully. Translations from the original documents of the eternal record can be misleading if not done carefully. For example, I refer to the word *stars* in the preceding passage. In the original Hebrew dictionary, the word *stars* is translated as *shining princes*. The inferred meaning is that these princes were considered to be in a special relationship like that of sons to a father. (Adam himself is referred to as a son of God.) It is quite evident that Adam was created and *not* born. In contrast, Jesus, the *first begotten* Son of God, was born and *not* created.

Sons of Adam could not possibly exist before Adam himself did. This makes the mystery clear that the creation of earth happened at the beginning of time area 2. Now we know that before the earth was created, there were other beings created by God—in this case, the shining princes! This exactly agrees with the first verse of the creation record as follows: "In the *beginning* God created the heaven: then the earth" (emphasis added). Therefore, the beginning must be a dividing line between time areas 1 and 2. And so it is, as we see in verse two: "And the earth had no form, and it was empty."

This brings up another mystery; why would God create an earth that was without form and empty? The answer is that God created heaven first, then earth, and then humankind! Some of these shining princes that existed before humankind became evil. Satan, for example,

3

was the first to sin, and other angelic beings followed him into sin, thereby becoming enemies of God and humankind.

Something must have happened to make God's creation "without form and empty." This agrees perfectly with the eternal record given by the Lord Jesus Christ in the New Testament: "I saw Satan fall from heaven like lightning." Now we know how the earth became formless and empty, and darkness was upon the face of the deep waters. Satan and *some* of the shining princes are *now* the powers of darkness. This darkness is the domain of the Devil. Darkness, which is also a symbol of spiritual blindness, is the opposite of light and truth. For by Him (God the Son, the living Word), were all things created that are in heaven and in earth, visible and invisible, whether they are thrones or dominions or principalities or powers: "all things were created by and for Christ. He existed before all other things, and by Him all things are sustained in their places."

We know these powers were created long before the earth was and that some followed Satan into sin and darkness. Satan was found after his fall, in the garden of Eden, as the serpent, the tempter of Eve and Adam. He was and is the Prince of the Power of the Air, the Destroyer; he is the Enemy of God and of humankind.

We can easily confirm these truths from the eternal record in the New Testament: "And you [you means *all* Christians, including us today], being dead in your sins and the carnality of your body: God has made alive together with Christ, having forgiven you all sins; canceling the writings of laws and regulations that was against us, which was opposed to us, and took them out of the way, by nailing them to His Cross." And having overcome the lawless principalities and powers lead by Satan, He made a show of them, openly triumphing over them in showing the world his death on the cross, and his resurrection the third day." These powers are very real and active in the affairs of human beings. Let us reference the record again to show this truth: "Humble yourselves therefore under the mighty hand of God, that he may exalt you in due time: casting all your care upon Him; for he cares for you. Be sober, be vigilant; for your adversary the Devil, as a roaring lion, walks about seeking whom he may devour: Whom resist: all the while standing fast in the faith [of God]." In the same record, we can read: "And there was a war in heaven: Michael and his angels fought against the dragon; and the dragon and his angels fought; and did not prevail, and neither was their place found anymore in heaven." This angelic war will happen in the future in another administration of time, but now we have the following admonition: "We wrestle not against flesh and blood, but against principalities, against powers, against the rulers of the darkness of this world, against Spiritual Wickedness in high places [or the heavenly places] ... Now the Spirit speaks expressly that in the latter times [today], some shall depart from the faith, giving heed to seducing spirits and doctrines of devils." We can understand that this condition exists in our world today. Our society is saturated with crime at all levels. The planet has wars of great bloodshed year after year. "The thoughts and intents of men's hearts were only evil continually [referring to humankind's condition before the great flood]." So it is today and gets worse daily. Our walk in this life is one of tribulation because we cannot see these powers that wage war against us.

What is our response? "Put on the whole Armour of God, that you may be able to withstand against the trickery of the Devil. Stand therefore having put on the belt of Truth, with the breastplate of righteousness, and on your feet preparation of the good news of peace. Above all take the shield of faith, protection against the fiery darts of the wicked. And take the helmet of Salvation, and the sword of the Spirit, which is the Word of God; praying always …"

Time Area 2

Time area 2 begins with "in the beginning." Humankind was *not* the beginning of creation; rather, human beings were created from the recreated earth, as is described in the eternal record. At some point in time, after heaven was created, the creation of earth began. The earth must have been very beautiful, even more than it is today. So what must we think when we read the next verse? "And the earth was without form and void; and darkness was upon the deep, and the Spirit of God moved on the face of the waters." Now we must have a problem understanding an earth that has no form and nothing in it! The earth was not created to be without form and empty! Again, from the eternal record of humankind, we read, "Thus says the Lord who created the heavens; God Himself that formed the earth and made it; he has established it, he did not create it in vain, He *formed* it to be inhabited: I am the Lord and there is no other!" (emphasis added). What happened then, that the earth was without form and void? From the record, we have this account, "I beheld Satan as lightning *fall from heaven*!" (emphasis added). We know the Lord recreated the earth, and we know that Satan had access to the garden of Eden; therefore, he must have been responsible for the damage to the earth. One of Satan's titles is Destroyer.

The sweet mystery of humankind begins here: "Let us make man in our own image, and in our likeness … and let him have Dominion over all Earth." Here is the *heart* of humankind's mystery: the image and likeness of God. Nowhere in the record can we find any statement that any other creature was made in the image and likeness of God! This statement must have upset some beings in the principalities, such as the other authorities and lords of the universe; for now these have brought unrighteousness into being. For example, the Bible discusses speaking to the king of Tyrus (the commercial system of earth in ages past), as if that king were human (which he is not; in this discourse he is Satan):

> Say to the prince of Tyrus; thus says the Lord God; because your heart is lifted up … you said you are a god, I sit in the seat of God … yet you are not a god, but a hypocrite, though you *want* to be God. You seal up the sum, full of wisdom and perfect in beauty.
>
> You have been in the garden of Eden [only Satan could have been in the garden of Eden, the garden of God, before Adam was created]; every precious stone was your covering, the sardius, topaz, the diamond, the beryl, the onyx … the workmanship of your services and bezels was prepared in you, in the

day you were *created* you were the anointed cherub that covers; and I have set you there.

You were upon the holy mountain of God. You were perfect in your ways from the day you were created, until iniquity [evil] was found in you. Your heart was lifted up because of your beauty, you have corrupted your wisdom by reason of your brightness: I will cast you to the ground, I will lay you before kings, that they can see you. You have defiled your sanctuaries by the multitude of your iniquities, by the lawlessness of your trading; therefore I will bring a fire from within you and it will devour you … to destruction on the earth, in sight of all that look at you.

Humankind and its mystery are unique. First, God made Adam from the very earth he inhabits. This is why the record calls him "an earthen vessel." Second, God breathed into Adam the breath of life. That life from an eternal God had to be immortal. Third,

God made him in his own image and likeness. Fourth, God gave Adam dominion (rule) over all of earth. Because of the temptations of Satan, Adam and his descendants lost all of his gifts, including immortality, the image and likeness of God, and the rule over earth. Satan exercises dominion over earth by using deceit to control a sinful society of human beings.

This just begins the mystery of humankind. The next part of this great mystery will later be revealed in the person of the *second Adam*. This revelation continues in time area 2.

2

The Woman Made from Man

God saw that it was not good for man to be alone. So God caused a deep sleep to fall upon Adam, and He took one of Adam's ribs, closed the flesh, and made a woman from the rib He had taken. When God presented her to Adam, Adam said, "This is bone from my bones, and flesh from my flesh." Now we have another mystery: man and woman are from the same flesh and bone; they should be the same, but they are different, and now they are together in a family unit. They are taken from the earth and, therefore, "earthy." They are bound to earth, subsisting on its produce, and nurtured by the water and air. Is it not a mystery? Adam was created from the dust of the earth, so he was an "earthen vessel." The woman, Eve, having been created from Adam, was also an earthen vessel. It should be of interest to us that ever since God made the family unit, Satan has been actively trying to destroy it.

Is woman a creation made from a creation? The eternal record states it this way; God made the woman from a man's bone and flesh. This is very different from an original creation, as it allows two to be one creation: "male and female created he them." So, all life on earth is male and female.

The man and woman's reproductive systems were now in place and beginning to produce human beings by natural birth. Adam's problems now came upon him without mercy. God placed Adam in the garden of Eden, a paradise, where everything a human being could want was there and free to use. He commanded Adam, "you can eat of every tree in the garden *except* the tree of the knowledge of good and evil: for in the day you eat of it you shall die" (emphasis added). But we find that there was a foreigner there, as well: the Enemy, the Devil, appeared as a Serpent and tempted Eve with a weapon he still uses against us today; he simply asked her if she wanted something more than paradise. She always wanted something more, not realizing she had to be disobedient to God to get it.

When Eve broke the law of God by taking of the forbidden tree, she became the first sinner of the human race; she realized that fact immediately. To show us the evilness of sin, Eve then became the willing servant of the Devil, the first sinner of all creation. She convinced Adam to take and eat of the tree, and in so doing, he joined her in death; death, then, came upon all humankind. The man freely and willfully made his decision, thereby becoming subject to another law of God. "What ever a person sows, he shall also reap."

Then the sentence was pronounced upon them by the Judge of all the Earth, God Himself: "You woman, will have tribulation bearing children. For your sake Adam, the earth is cursed, it will bear thorns and thistles to you, and by the sweat of your face shall you eat of it." As bad as the sentence was, they lost much more: they *lost* immortal life, the image and likeness of God, and dominion over the Earth. Now we know the answer to why humankind has so much trouble. Dominion over earth, because of Adam's sin, has now been forfeited to Satan, who obtained it by fraud. Satan exercises dominion by deceiving naturally sinful people.

God will *not* be defeated. God will regain everything the first Adam lost! He has told us how He will win the battle of good against evil; He will do it with the promise made to Eve that she will bear the *seed of the woman*! As is written in the eternal record, "I will put enmity between your seed and the Devil, Your Seed will bruise the head of the Devil; and he will bruise the heel of your seed [offspring]." This is a mystery. Why would God tell the woman about a seed not yet existing? Eve had not yet delivered a child. The reason is that Adam failed the test and fell into sin, taking all of humankind into sin as well and losing everything God created for His glory. Now we can think of a man on earth who was to be a child made of a woman—a man who is called the *second Adam*. Why? Because the first Adam lost the battle against sin. The second Adam, from God *and* a woman, must regain everything the first man lost. He tells us in his own words: "The son of man is come to seek and to save that which was lost." The title used here is repeated many times in the word of God.

Eve must have thought the promise would be fulfilled by her firstborn, Cain (a tiller of the ground) for she said, "I have gotten a man from the Lord." Then her second son came, who was named Abel (a keeper of the sheep). This is not an accident, for the eternal record shows us two types of man: Cain, the sinner of the earth, and Abel, a type of spiritual son of the promised seed. Cain demonstrates the awfulness of his sinful soul by murdering his only brother because of selfish jealousy. Do we see the picture here? Adam's firstborn was a sinner and a murderer of the son born of a woman. That would have been the end of humankind if God had not said a son made of a woman will deal a death blow to the serpent, the Devil. God sees to it that Eve has a second son to replace the first one lost to sin. That second son is a *type* of the second Adam, Jesus of Nazareth, the Lord from heaven.

Here Is a Great Mystery of the Ages

Here is a great mystery of the ages from the eternal record: "When you read this writing you should understand; the Mystery of Christ, which God did not reveal to men of past ages; but is now revealed to his holy apostles and prophets by his spirit: that the Gentiles should be fellow heirs and members of the same body in Christ, and partakers of his promise made through the Gospel." God's plan was in place all along, as intended, and now it shows us its mystery: Eve's third son was called Seth (which means *appointed*). He was to be the promised seed instead of Abel.

In Seth, we see the first of many substitutions in the line of the *promised son*. These substitutions continue through time for thousands of years. Each and every substitution in the ancestry of our Lord Jesus Christ has a special meaning and reason for happening; they show us that the One who went to the cross was the only begotten Son of God and not just any man who came through the ages by chance. God is very careful to list in His Word, the eternal record, the genealogy of Eve's seed. It is quite lengthy, so I will list just a few here to show the awesome power of God in bringing His Son into the world: Abraham's son Isaac was favored instead of Ishmael, Jacob instead of Esau, Judah instead of Reuben, and Solomon instead of David and Bathsheba's firstborn son; this continued all the way through the centuries, into the days of the birth of Christ: the Holy Spirit was the chosen father instead of Joseph, the husband of Mary, who was a descendent of David, who was a descendent of the tribe of Judah instead of the tribe the firstborn, Reuben, who was also a descendent of the woman Eve, who was made from Adam the sinner.

The record tells us that "God sent forth His son made of a woman." That woman was Mary, the daughter of another woman, *Israel*. Clearly, our Lord Jesus Christ is a son of Israel through the tribe of Judah, and his Father is almighty God. His rightful title is The Lion of the Tribe Of Judah.

3

The Mystery of Iniquity

In Time Area 2

Remembering the ancients, we must remember that there was only one race on earth; the whole race was of one language and one speech. They decided to build a city. They said *let us build a tower that will reach to heaven; and let us make us a name, lest we be scattered abroad upon the whole face of the earth.* From the record, we know the Lord said, "behold the people are one, they have the same language, and this they begin to do: and nothing will be restrained from them, which they have imagined to do. Let us go down and confound their language that they will not understand each others speech." So the Lord scattered them abroad upon all the earth. Then they stopped building the city and the tower. Therefore, the name of this tower is Babel, which means "confusion." From this word comes the name Babylon. This is the first time the name appears in the eternal record, but it is not the last. The name indicates darkness (with evil and Mystery), which it represents.

We now know that the flood that removed the great mass of sinners from earth, did *not* remove the lawlessness of humankind; the mystery of iniquity is still working among human beings and will continue until it is destroyed by God. When we look at the record for the end times, we see that the system that began after the flood is the mysterious political, commercial, and religious system that we are in today and that we will be in this same system until the very end of humankind's rule, which will end before the Lord's kingdom on earth begins.

The same record continues to describe the people of this system in the tribulation of the end times by explaining, "They did not regret nor turn away from their murders, nor of their drug addiction, or of their fornication, or of their thefts." Even as I write this, the news has come out of Pakistan: "two suicide bombers exploded two bombs at a Christian church, killing 68, and wounding more ..." We can now realize that modern human beings have, just as was predicted, become like they were in the days before Noah's ark floated away. The racial issue has become a weapon that one race uses against another in this mystery system, even as nation wars against nation. This was also predicted: "race will rise against race, and kingdom against kingdom ... and there will be famines, and deadly diseases, and earthquakes in unusual places." We are very aware of this condition on earth today. Does God favor one race over another? Of course not! We see from the record that God has said, "After this I beheld a great multitude which no man can number, of *all* nations and people and tongues; stand before the throne and before the Lamb [Jesus Christ] ... and cried with a loud voice saying, Salvation is of our God which sits upon the throne and to the Lamb" (emphasis added). Certainly God does not favor one race over another. So-called *racism* is a human device used for evil purposes. Whenever human beings are against their fellow human beings for any reason, we will have a problem.

4

The Mystery of Israel

After the great flood, in repopulating the earth, humankind became evil in rejecting God and was scattered abroad as a result. However, God's program could not be defeated, which was to send the seed of the woman, the second Adam, to earth so that He could be the redeemer of sinful man. So God called a man named Abram (meaning high father), from among one race, and began to build a race from him that would follow God in obedience; from this race he could fulfill his promise to the woman that she would indeed bear the promised seed.

As the eternal record further reveals, "Now the Lord had said to Abram, leave your country and your kindred, and go to a land that I will show you: and I will make of you a Great Nation, and I will bless you, and make your name great; and you shall be a blessing: and I will bless those who bless you, and curse those who curse you, and in *you* shall

all families of the earth be blessed" (emphasis added). The blessing comes not from Abram, but from God, *to* Abram's offspring down through the ages. One man who became a race of people, the promised seed, made from a woman, was also the seed of Abram (whose name was later changed to Abraham, meaning father of a multitude). This seed gave way to the Savior of all who will receive Him. The history of this special race is given in minute and precise detail in the eternal word of God, over a period of more than four thousand years of humankind's residence on this globe.

There can be no reasonable doubt that God has done exactly as He said he would. Let us then briefly list some of the high points of time and history: Abraham believed the promise made to him by God and acted on that promise. We might ask about the mystery of how Abram knew God was talking to him. The eternal record of humankind answers, "Salvation is by the grace of God thru faith, and that not of yourselves, it is the gift of God: not of works, lest anyone should boast." It becomes obvious that God would have given Abram the faith he needed to believe, for it says, "and Abraham believed God, and that was accounted to him for righteousness."

From Abraham came Isaac, Jacob, Judah, then on to David, and then Solomon, and finally on to Mary, a descendant of David, and to Jesus her firstborn, by God the Holy Spirit. Please remember that the woman Eve was made from a man. Just as great a miracle we find within the eternal record: "But when the fullness of time was come, God sent forth *his* Son made of a woman! Made under the Law, to redeem those that were under the law, that we might receive the *adoption of sons*" (emphasis added).

The history of women is also a part of the eternal record; we find women in most interesting places in history. After Eve, the wife of Abraham, Sarah, was delivered of Abraham's son, Isaac, when she was past the natural age to bear children. Abraham himself was ninety-nine years of age at the time. She was the grandmother of Jacob, whose wife, Rachel, changed history by finding a way for Esau, the eldest of her twin sons, to be tricked into selling his birthright to Jacob for just a hot meal when he was hungry. Because of her, the Messiah, Jesus, was a descendent of Jacob and of his son, Judah.

Jacob fathered twelve sons by four women. These twelve sons became a great nation that God called Israel. This people Israel is also called a woman, who is by Jacob called, "the Moon with a Crown of 12 Stars: Israel declared to be God's Wife." As such, God's Son, Jesus of Nazareth, was born of the woman Mary. But much more than that, He is called son of the *woman Israel*, as she is described in the eternal record.

The time period of this picture begins with the cross and continues up until the middle of the tribulation. The Bible prophesies,

> And there appeared a great wonder in heaven; a woman clothed with the sun, and the moon under her feet, and upon her head a crown of 12 stars. And she being with child, cried, travailing in birth, and pained to be delivered. And there appeared another wonder in heaven; a great red Dragon, having 7 heads and 10 horns, and Seven Crowns upon his heads. And his tail drew one third

of the angels, of heaven and cast them to the earth: and the Dragon stood before the woman which was ready to be delivered, to devour her child as soon as it was born. And she brought forth a man child, who was to rule all nations with a rod of Iron: and her child was caught up to God and to his throne. We know this is the birth, crucifixion, death, burial, and resurrection of the Lord Jesus Christ: we are still waiting for him to take his rightful rule and reign of over all the earth ... And the woman fled into the wilderness, where she has a place of protection prepared for her by God, that they should feed her there three and one half years. Remembering that the Dragon [Satan] was attempting to destroy both Israel and Her Child; failing on both counts, he continues the war just the same, but now he must carry the war against the Son of God; all the way to heaven.

The record tells us about that future war. "And there was a war in heaven: Michael and his angels fought against the dragon and his angels. The dragon and his angels did not prevail, neither was their place found any more in heaven. And the great dragon was cast out, that old serpent, called the Devil and Satan, who deceives the whole world: he was cast out into the earth, and his angels were cast out with him."

And I heard a loud voice from heaven saying; salvation, and strength, and the kingdom of our God and the power of his Christ is come: for the accuser of our brethren is cast down, which accused them before our God day and night. And they overcame the destroying accuser, by the blood of the Lamb, and by the word of their testimony, and they did not love their lives unto death." Woe to those who inhabit the earth, for the devil is come down to you, having great wrath, because he knows he has but a short time."

Seeing that he was cast to the earth, the Devil persecuted the woman that brought forth the man-child. And to the woman were given two wings of a great eagle so she could fly into her place in the wilderness to be nourished. Satan then continued his war against Israel by sending his armies against her, but God defended her and destroyed Satan's forces. Failing that, Satan made war against her offspring, who kept the commandments of God and have the testimony of Jesus Christ.

It is easy to see the Enemy's persistence in his attempts to destroy God's people. He never wins, but he never gives up—at least not until the Lord casts him into the bottomless pit. We are warned about our Enemy in the letters to the churches. For example, one of the letters tells us, "Be sober, be vigilant; because your adversary the devil, as a roaring lion, walks about seeking whom he may devour: whom resist steadfast in the faith of God, knowing that the same afflictions are accomplished in your brethren that are in the world." The way to win, according to this same letter, is to "submit yourself to God. Resist the devil and he will flee from you."

The Mystery of Israel's Elect Four Sons

The birth order of human beings within a family is very important; that order determines the destiny of each of us. The first son will become the ruler of his brothers and receive a double portion of his father's fortune, including the blessing of being an *ancestor* of the promised seed of the woman. These three rights went to the first-born. This was a law from God in Israel and was strictly adhered to. (The exception to this law is ordained by Divine choice; laws can and will be altered according to His *purpose*).

Israel's twelve sons were born in this order: first was Reuben, whose name means "see a son"; second was Simeon, whose name means "hearing"; third was Levi, whose name means "joined"; fourth was Judah, whose name means "praise"; fifth was Dan, whose name means "judge"; sixth was Napthali, whose name means "wrestling"; seventh was Gad, whose name means "a troop" or "a multitude"; eighth was Asher, whose name means "happiness"; ninth was Issachar, whose name means "reward"; tenth was Zebulun, whose name means "dwelling"; eleventh was Joseph, whose name means "adding"; and twelfth was Benjamin, whose name means "son of my power."

Four of these brothers are a mystery. Reuben was born to be great among his brothers, ruling among them, but something happened when he became old enough to make adult decisions; he chose to commit a grievous sin against God, and against his father. He committed adultery with his father's harem. God took all the blessings of the firstborn away and gave them to the number four son, Judah. Therefore, Judah became the first among many brethren and would be praised among them. The next great son was number five, Dan, who was to become the judge of Israel. Next was the eleventh, Joseph, who was to become blessed beyond measure by God, who does all things according to His own will and purpose.

Joseph was never guilty of any wrongdoing. He also was the son his father favored. Born of the wife that Jacob loved, Joseph was hated by his brothers because they could not commit wrongs without him knowing it. Further, Joseph reported their wrongs to his father. When the opportunity came for his brothers to get even, they sold him to a passing caravan and then lied, claiming that they knew nothing about his disappearance. Many years later, they found out that Joseph was alive and well in Egypt, even the chief prince; he was ruler over all except for the king himself.

Conditions of the time required the brothers to go into Egypt, where Joseph revealed his true identity to them. They were astounded when they found out he had forgiven them for their crime, returning to them blessings instead.

God blessed Joseph greatly, giving him an Egyptian wife and two sons, each of whom became a great tribe in Israel. We must note that Joseph's wife was not of the Jewish race. Since Joseph is a picture of Jesus Christ, his wife represents Jesus' bride, the church. So Joseph, whose name, again, means "adding," added his two sons, Manasseh and Ephraim, to the house of Israel. Similarly, Jesus, of the tribe of Judah (meaning, again, "the king"), added his gentile bride to Himself and to the kingdom of God. The church was and is built of both Jews and Gentiles, so now the total number of tribes is fourteen.

After being delivered from Egypt, Israel moved into the land promised to Abraham. It is easy to see here that Joseph was a type of God's son, being without sin and preferred above his brethren and, further, being given all the power in the universe, second only to God the Father.

The mystery does not end here; rather, it gets deeper as we find that these four great sons become prevalent in the future of all humankind. The great four are: Joseph, the man of God; Dan, the judge; Reuben, the sacrifice; and Judah, the king. Each one of these tribes represents the Lord Jesus Christ in a special way:

	Dan the Judge	
Joseph the Man	The Tabernacle of God	Judah the King
	Reuben the Sacrifice	

We see the picture here: Jesus, the perfect man and rightful King of Israel, came to earth and was sacrificed for the sins of people. Then He was raised from the dead to be the judge of all the earth. We see the above pattern repeated many times in the eternal record:

	God, Eagle, Judge, Dan	
God, Man, Joseph	God's Throne	God, King, Lion, Judah
	God, Ox, Calf, Sacrifice, Reuben	

This arrangement in the eternal record has great meaning for interpreting the prophetic secrets of God and humankind. All four of the sons represent a picture of the four ministries of Jesus the Christ. First, He is God the creator. Second, He is God, the Son of Man. Third, He is God, King of Israel. Fourth, He is the accepted sacrifice for sin: God the Lamb of God.

The nation of Israel exists because of the covenant made with Abraham, a covenant that persisted for thousands of years, right up to the death, burial, and resurrection of the Lord Jesus Christ. Many do *not* understand. The covenant was annulled, but it was not canceled! This means that all of Abraham's promises will be fulfilled now and in the future. We see this picture in the eternal record: "And before the throne there was a sea of glass like a crystal: and in the midst of the throne, and round about it: four living creations ... and the first was like Lion, second like a Calf, and the third like a Man and the fourth like an Eagle." This describes the redeemed Israel of all ages in one picture.

There is a time frame we call the *gap*. We live in that gap today. The eternal record calls it "The Times of The Gentiles." Gentiles consist of all nationalities other than Jews (Israel). History confirms this statement. For example, on May 15, 1948, the United Nations gave those Jews who had returned to the land of Israel national sovereignty. Many powers have tried to dislodge them since and are still trying. During this time of hatred of Israel, they have been protected through numerous wars and battles waged by their neighbors. These conditions will remain until the end of a time period called "the great tribulation."

The mystery is that the world at large is unaware that Israel will never be removed from its land or from earth itself by any power, no matter how great. The future does contain much tribulation and sorrow for Israel. We need to understand that the whole globe will also have it, and at the same time. The eternal record states, "for then shall be great tribulation, such as was not since the beginning of the world to this time, no, nor ever shall be. And except those days should be shortened, there should *no flesh* be saved: but for the elect's [God's people of all nationalities] sake, those days shall be shortened" (emphasis added)

Israel's survival is guaranteed by God Himself. But Israel will go through a terrible time for seven years, with great numbers of its people dying in that time. The conditions that cause this tribulation are listed in the record as follows: first, a false "messiah" will appear on earth, and he will represent himself to be God. The earth will give him universal rule over all nations. (He is also called the beast, or the beastly man, also known as the Antichrist). He will be the commander-in-chief of all military forces on earth. He will go about the planet, conquering and destroying all his opposition. He will change the laws of all nations so that the universal law will be "one race only". Second, his government will confiscate all private wealth. He will distribute it to certain of those whom he chooses. Third, his government will be a *one-source monopoly*. His government will own, control, and regulate all commerce, especially food and energy. Fourth, he will require *all* to worship him. The eternal record calls him "the *man of sin*, showing himself as god" (emphasis added). He will be *the* sworn enemy of Israel, seeking to destroy not only the nation but all who will not worship him. It will be the worst time in the history of humankind. "Peace" will cease to exist. Then, what will naturally follow the wars he makes will be military wars and wars between individuals, the killing one of another. This will cause food production to nearly cease. Then will come famine, starvation, disease, and death.

The forerunner of these conditions is here now; it is called "the beginning of sorrows." From the eternal record, we read, "Take heed that no one deceives you, there will be many coming in my name proclaiming themselves to be [the messiah] … for races shall rise against each other by their waring kingdoms; and there shall be famines, diseases, and earthquakes in different places: and all these things are only the Beginning of sorrows that are coming on this earth."

We are also warned to *watch* for these things, as they have now begun to happen throughout the world. In our day, we find there is an endless search for peace over all the earth, even to the ridiculous point of fighting war after war in the name of seeking peace. This mystery of war in the name of peace should warn us of the nature of the time in which we live today. To quote the eternal record, "they say peace, peace when there is *no* peace" (emphasis added). There is an endless rhetoric about the effort to sign peace treaties—sign this for that, and do this for that, and so on. If even a small treaty is signed, it is soon violated. Humankind has now fallen into a state of confusion and sorrow that leads to the great tribulation. This tribulation will be so great that no flesh would survive; thankfully, however, those days of death and disaster are limited in number.

5

The Mystery of Humankind's Numbers

The eternal record uses special numbers in special ways to send messages about great truths. The common modern system uses the base ten. There are other systems in use. Some are used by our people of science to define and create complex machines that we use every day.

Numbers According to the Eternal Record

One

The number one refers to the beginning and signifies: the one and only true God, the Almighty Creator of the universe. This is abundantly evident in the record, where God gives us some examples: "I am Alpha and Omega. The first and the last, the beginning and the ending says the Lord, which is, and which was, and is to come, the almighty." It is easy to see that number one expands and is included in an infinite series of numbers, without end. There is this fascinating statement made just preceding: "… from Jesus Christ who is the faithful witness, and the first *begotten* of the dead, and the prince of the kings of the earth: to him that loved us and washed us from our sins in his own blood" (emphasis added). Here is another: "If you have seen me, you have seen the Father … I [God] and my Father [God] are *one*" (emphasis added). Again, the record states, "I am the way, the truth, and the life: no man comes to the Father but by me."

Two

The number two refers to the Father and the Son. The record states, "God the Father was in Christ reconciling the world to himself … God said to the Son, 'Your throne O God, is forever and ever: a scepter of righteousness is the scepter of your kingdom.'" Number two also speaks of Adam the first and those things, like him, that are made of the earth, earthy, or having an earthy nature. It also refers to the second Adam, made of a woman (the Virgin), her firstborn son is the Lord from heaven. So it also means having a heavenly nature. From

the record, we can read: "As *we* have borne
the image of the earthly, *we* shall also bear
the image of the heavenly" (emphasis added).
Note: in this passage, find six pairs: two men,
two orders of men, two natures of men, two
images of men, two kinds of resurrections of
men, and two final conditions of men. God
gives us the victory over death through the
second man, our Lord Jesus Christ.

Three

The number three refers to the triune God.
According to the first book of the record, "the
Spirit [of God] moved upon the face of deep
waters," and God said, "let *us* make man in
our image after our likeness, and let them have
dominion … over all the earth." So we see
that a human being is in three parts, as the
record tells us, "I pray your whole spirit and
soul and body, be preserved without blame
until the coming of our Lord Jesus Christ.
Faithful is the one who calls you, who also will
do it." So it is clear that just as God is one in
three persons, His creation, human beings, are
one in three as well. From the eternal record
to the assembly of Christians, we read, "I

desire that you come together in agreement, finding the riches of assured understanding, to acknowledge the Mystery of God, and of the Father, and of Christ: For in him are hidden all the treasures of wisdom and knowledge."

These mysteries can be known by those who search for them through the giver of knowledge, the Lord Jesus Christ. He reveals them to us through the word of God, the Holy Scriptures. They are, as we say, the eternal record of humankind. How do we know that we have the authority to do this? It is recorded more than once, in both the Old and New Testaments:

> You have heard of the administration of the grace of God which is given to me for ministry to you; how that by revelation from God, he made known to me the Mystery; as I wrote before briefly, when you read this, you may understand my knowledge in the Mystery of Christ: which in other Ages, was not made known to the sons of men, as it is now revealed to his holy apostles and prophets by his Spirit. That the Non Jews [that

are in Christ], should be fellow heirs
and of the same body, and partakers
of his promise in Christ by the
Gospel.

And again, speaking to His own, Jesus said,
"Unto you it is given to know the Mysterys
of the kingdom of God: but to those outside
the kingdom, we speak to them in parables."
And again we read from the Old Testament,
"Whom shall God teach knowledge? And to
whom shall he make to understand doctrine?
Those who are weaned from milk [of the
Word], and are away from the breasts." We
are given the admonition that "we must grow
in grace and in the knowledge of our Lord and
Savior Jesus Christ. To him be glory both now
and forever, Amen."

We want to know the mysteries of God,
humankind, and the world God created for
us. The record also tells us, "Go therefore and
teach all nations, baptizing them in the name
of [God] the Father, and of [God] the Son,
and of the [God] the Holy Spirit." It is most
regrettable that so many do not want even to
hear these things, let alone to know them.

Four

The number four refers to the next great mystery, which is the recorded first physical death in the human race. Abel, the fourth human being born on this earth, was a keeper of sheep. He brought the firstborn of his flock and offered it as a sacrifice to God, which was accepted. His sacrifice demonstrated an image of the Good Shepherd, our Lord Jesus Christ, who was rejected, hated, and put to death on the cross. He was, of course, an acceptable sacrifice to God. We also see here that Abel is left out of the genealogy of Adam! Why? He is left out to prove that the Lord Jesus Christ did not have the sinful nature of Adam and to prove that Christ is the only way, the only truth, and the only life. Number four follows three, Just as the Savior, the Son of God, the Son of Man (second Adam), follows with His power to save a lost humankind.

Only God's salvation can deliver humankind from eternal death.

Now we see what these numbers mean: one is God the Father, two is God the Son, three is God the Holy Spirit, four is God the

Savior, five is the redeemed people of God, six is the judgment of the world, and seven is the kingdom of God.

Five

The number five represents our gift of eternal life through the grace of God. After the cross of Christ, we are told in the eternal record, "By grace are you saved thru faith; and that not because you have merit: it is the gift of God: not of your works, lest any one should boast. For we are his workmanship in Christ Jesus created to good works, which God has before ordained that we should walk in them."

There could not be grace without the sacrifice of the Son. Note that this number has a great application in the record because it refers to the fifth dispensation in God's plan of redemption. Included in this plan is the fact that five, according to the record, is the number of God's dwelling: "In [Christ], you [His body, the true church] are also built together for a Habitation of God thru the Spirit."

We saw the same picture before: God's tabernacle is in the center of the four camps of Israel. God plus four camps equals five. We can also see God as the Son of Man, walking among human beings for a little while as He prepared for His death, burial, and resurrection. This is a great mystery concerning Christ and the church. The eternal Word of God gives this explanation: "God was in Christ, reconciling the world to himself, and has committed to us, (the Church), the Word of reconciliation." The church has been assigned a work of faith, and that is, in essence, the ministry of the Word of God. The church on the corner is a building for ministry, but the people are the church that Jesus built!

The key is to begin with the building of His church: the cornerstone comes first, and then comes the foundation. Great rocks have been used throughout time as material for buildings, and, referring to Jesus, the record advises, "On this Rock, I will build *my* church, and the gates of hell shall not prevail against it" (emphasis added). The record continues, "For He is our peace, who has made both Jew and Gentile One, and are built upon the foundation of the apostles and prophets, Jesus Christ himself being the chief cornerstone." Compare the following statement: "You brothers know how that when all our [Jewish] fathers were delivered from the bondage of Egypt, and were under the cloud [of God], and all passed through the sea, and all were immersed to Moses in the cloud and in the sea; and all of them ate the same spiritual meat; all drank of the same spiritual drink: for they drank of that spiritual Rock that followed them: and that Rock was Christ. But with many of them, God was not well pleased: for they were overthrown in the wilderness. Why? Because some of them turned away from God, and went after the pleasures of this world. So we see that the same Savior that followed them; is the one that built the Gentile church on Himself, He put them both together into *one*" (emphasis added). This brings us to the mystery of the seven churches.

Mystery of the Seven Churches:
A War against the Mystery of Iniquity

The Enemy of God and humankind, Satan, has been at war with us since the garden of Eden. The church is one of his battlefields. The Word of God reports as follows:

I John [the apostle] was in the Island of Patmos being exiled for testifying the truth of the Word of God, and Jesus Christ. I was caught up to heaven on the Lord's Day, and heard behind me a great voice, as of a trumpet, Saying, I am Alpha and Omega, the first and the last; What you see write in a book, and send it to the Seven churches which are in Asia: to Ephesus, Smyrna, Pergamos, Thyatira, Sardis, Philadelphia, and Laodicea. And I turned to see the voice that spoke with me, and I saw seven golden candlesticks; and in their center; one like the Son of man, clothed with a garment down to his feet, and having a golden belt about his chest. His head and his hair were white like wool, as white as snow; and his eyes were as a flame of fire; and his feet like fine brass, as if they burned in a furnace; and his voice as the sound of many waters. And he had in his right hand seven stars: and out of his mouth went a sharp two edged sword, and his countenance shined bright as the sun.

And when I saw him I fell at his feet as dead. And he laid his right hand upon me, saying, Fear not; I am the first and the last: I am he that lives and was dead; and behold I am alive forevermore, Amen; and have the keys of hell and of death. Write the things which you have seen [the resurrected Savior, Jesus Christ] and the things which are [the seven churches] and the things which shall take place after them [the Day of the Lord, the tribulation]. The *mystery* of the seven stars, and the seven golden candlesticks. The seven stars are the messengers of the seven churches: and the seven candlesticks are the seven churches. (emphasis added)

There is great misunderstanding as to *why* there are just seven churches given in this record, when there were at least twenty-four local churches existing at the time of John's writing. (Think of the number that exist today.) That secret is revealed as we examine the messages to the churches themselves.

Briefly, we must look at these seven as *typical* of *all* churches of the time period that began with the formation of His church and that persists through the present, ending at Christ's second coming. Remember that the church is in a *battle* with Satan, whose strategy is to deceive in order to destroy. From the record to the church, we can read,

> For I am jealous over you with godly jealousy: for I have espoused you to one husband, that I may present you as a chaste virgin to Christ. But I fear, lest by any means, as the serpent deceived Eve through his trickery, so your Minds should be corrupted from the simplicity that is in Christ. For if he that comes among you preaches another Jesus, whom We have Not preached, or if you receive another spirit, which you have not received, or another gospel which you have not accepted, Beware ... For those are *false apostles*, deceitful workers,

Transforming themselves into the likeness, of the apostles of Christ. They have a *form* of godliness, but they and their works deny the power of God, from such turn away. And no marvel; for Satan himself is Transformed into the likeness of an angel of light. Therefore, it is no great thing if Satan's Ministers also be Disguised as ministers of righteousness; whose end shall be according to their works.

This is the real danger to the church, and the *Lord Jesus Christ Himself shows it to us*. Here are the results of the battle according to His evaluation of each of the seven churches.

With regard to Ephesus, the Lord says, "I have something against you because you left your first love [The Lord Himself]: Remember from where you fell, and repent, and do the first works; or else I will come to you quickly and remove your candlestick out of its place. He that has an ear, let him hear what the spirit says to the churches; to those who overcome; I will give to eat of the tree of life, which is in the midst of the paradise of God."

We know that this falling away was propagated by the Enemy, Satan, through the work of his agents who were transplanted into the church fellowship. He knew to send imitation Christians into the group, as they eventually get strong enough to take over the leadership and then the rule.

If we followed with the second church listed here (Smyrna), we would lose temporal continuity, for Smyrna is the one who *goes* into the tribulation at the exact time Philadelphia *leaves* earth to meet the Lord in the air. Smyrna is then left on earth to preach the gospel of the kingdom. We must be careful to note that the membership of this glorious church is made of 144,000 Jews of all the tribes of Israel.

The record gives a requirement as follows: "And when he had called to him his twelve disciples, he gave them power against unclean spirits to cast them out, and to heal all manner of sickness and all kinds of disease … and he commanded them saying; 'Go not into the way of the gentiles, nor to any city of the Samaritans enter not: but rather go to the lost sheep of the house of Israel and as you go, preach, saying the kingdom of heaven is at hand.'" This gospel

is the *gospel of the kingdom*. The gospel of the
kingdom has *never* been preached by the true
church since the cross and the resurrection of
the Lord. Instead, the true church preaches,
"believe on the Lord Jesus Christ and you
will be saved, and your house." This gospel is
for everyone in our dispensation. We rejoice to
note that there will be a *future* preaching of the
kingdom gospel as follows:

To the church of the tribulation (Smyrna),
God The Son, preaches,

> Then [in the tribulation] they shall
> deliver you up to be afflicted, and
> shall kill you: and you shall be *hated*
> *of all nations for my name's sake.* And
> then many shall be offended, and
> will betray and hate one another.
> And many false prophets shall
> stand up and deceive many. And
> because sin and lawlessness shall
> abound, the love of many will grow
> cold. But he that endures to the end
> of Israel's age [the seven years of
> tribulation], the same will be saved:
> And this *gospel of the kingdom*, shall
> be preached in all the world for a

witness to *all* nations, and then the
end of that age of tribulation will
come. (emphasis added)

So then, according to *time*, the order would
be: Ephesus, Pergamos, Thyatira, Sardis,
Philadelphia, the false church Laodicea, and
Smyrna.

To the church of Pergamos, God The Son,
preaches,

I know your works and where you
dwell, even where Satan's seat of
power is; and you hold fast my name,
and have not denied my faith ... but
I have this against you; because
you have those there that hold
and teach the doctrine of Balaam,
which led the people into coveting
and practicing sins of fornication
and Idolatry. You also have those
who practice the false doctrine of
a master ruling over the assembly.
This I hate: repent; or else I will
come and Fight against them with
the Sword of my mouth. He that has
an ear; let him hear what the spirit

says to the churches; to him that overcomes will I give to eat of the hidden manna, and will give him a white stone, and in the stone, a new name written which no man knows except him who receives it.

(Note: white is symbolic of righteousness, and the stone speaks of the cornerstone of His church, the Lord Jesus Christ, and almighty God, the Rock of Ages.)

Here we see Satan's plan of attack *against* the church: In this early age, there were no other churches near it, and they did not yet have the written Scriptures, as we do; the New Testament Scriptures were still being written. The church had to depend upon traveling apostles for instruction on church policy and practice.

They were depending on representatives of God [the Apostles], for guidance.

Satan sent in one of his false prophets; in this case, he chose an ancient prophet who preached a *similar* doctrine and who caused great harm to Israel: his name was Balaam. His doctrine was essentially what we find in some churches today: it's all right to live like the world, and you can even commit adultery, because God will forgive you for it. This is a lie, of course. Satan's throne has always been the source of lies. The people followed Balaam and were condemned for that sin, by the Lord Himself.

To the church of Thyatira, God The Son preaches,

> I know your works, and love, and service, and faith, and your patience, and your works; and the last will be more than the first. Notwithstanding I have a few things against you, because you are allowing that woman Jezebel, who calls herself a prophetess, to Teach and to seduce my servants to commit fornication, and to eat things sacrificed to idols ... I gave her time to repent, but she would not. Behold, I will cast her into a bed, and those who commit adultery with her into Great Tribulation, unless they repent of their deeds. And I will kill her children with death; and all the churches will know that I am the

One who searches the Minds and Hearts: and I will give to every one of you according to your works.

But I say to you and the rest in Thy-a-ti-ra, as many as have not this doctrine, and which have not known the depths of Satan as they speak it. I will put upon you no other burden: but that which you have, hold fast till I come. And he that overcomes, and keeps My works to the end: to him I will give power over the nations: and he will rule them with a rod of iron … And I will give him the morning star. He that has an ear let him hear what the spirit says to the churches.

Satan then used another weapon, a woman, who called herself a minister of the Word. She was strictly forbidden to be teaching in the church, and she taught the church to be in fellowship with idolaters and to commit fornication. This brought swift condemnation from the Lord. This practice continues today; it is called by different names, but it does damage just the same.

To the church of Sardis, God the Son preaches,

> These things says He that has the seven spirits of God, who has his eyes like a flame of fire, and his feet are like fine brass; I know your works, that you claim a name that you are living, while you are Dead: be watchful, and strengthen the things which remain, that are ready to die: for I have not found your works perfect before God. He that overcomes, shall be clothed in white; and I will not blot out his name from the book of life, but will confess his name before my Father and before his angels. He that has an ear let him hear what the spirit says to the churches.

Satan attacked this church with something called "doctrines of devils." The record reports, "For the time will come when *some* will depart from the faith of God, giving heed to seducing spirits and doctrines of devils" (emphasis added). A doctrine of a devil may be defined as any doctrine *contrary* to the Word of God. These false doctrines are very cleverly fashioned so they appear to be close to the truth. Be not deceived; close is *not* good enough.

To the church of Laodicea, God the Son preaches,

> These things says the Amen, the faithful and true witness, the one who Began the creation of God: I know your works that you are neither cold nor hot: I would that you were cold or hot. So then because you are neither one: I will spit you out of my mouth. You say you are rich and have need of nothing, and don't know that you are wretched, miserable, poor, blind and naked … As many as I love, I rebuke and chasten: be zealous therefore and repent. To him that overcomes, will I grant to sit with me in my throne, even as I also overcame and sit down with my Father in his throne.

Satan sent in his most talented ministers to fight against this church, which is typical of many churches in our day. Yes, Satan has ministers;

they come into the church with doctrines that say we need to hire the best and most educated ministers to direct the work and programs the people need. We need fund drives to increase our capacity to build large, fine buildings, so that we can attract the wealthy to our congregation. The wealthy will attract more like them, and we will have even more wealth for our programs of feeding the poor, providing shelter for the homeless, educating our young people, providing them with gymnasiums so they compete with other schools in sports, and so on. And we need to change our teachings to conform to the modern times we live in. We do not need outdated doctrines that read like fables, such as the fable that Christ is divine and rose from the dead. Every intelligent person knows that is impossible. These ministers actually exist! Here is the record: "For there are false apostles, deceitful workers, transforming themselves into a likeness of the apostles of Christ. And no marvel; for Satan himself is transformed so as to appear to be an angel of light. Therefore it is no great thing if his ministers are also transformed to imitate ministers of righteousness: whose end shall be according to their works." Again, in the words of our Savior, we read, "Not everyone that says to me, Lord, Lord, shall enter into the kingdom of heaven; but he that does the will of my Father which is in heaven. Many will say to me in that Day, Lord, Lord, have we not prophesied in your name? And in your name have cast out devils, and in your name done many wonderful works? And then will I profess to them, I Never knew you; depart from me you that work unrighteousness."

Before we continue, may I point out that the *working* of Satan within the churches is clearly seen? His working is seen in the politics of humankind, specifically with regard to *false doctrine* and *unscriptural practice*! Five of the seven churches are types of wrong religious practice that have been in the society of humankind for two thousand years. But also understand that in spite of Satan's war against the church, he will not win! For next we will see the *true church* of the Lord Jesus Christ. In His own words, Jesus says, "On this rock [Himself], I will build my church, and the Gates of Hell shall not prevail against it." The gates of hell refers to Satan and his agents, who are themselves at the very gates: the entry into hell.

We are told, "Be sober and vigilant; because your adversary Satan like a roaring lion, walks around seeking someone to destroy." Satan the Destroyer keeps trying, but he *cannot overcome Christ's church*! The next church is the true church, which is His body: Christ will come for it soon.

To the church of Philadelphia, God, The son preaches,

> These things says he that is holy, he that is true, he that has the key of David, he that opens and no man shuts; and shuts and no man opens; I know your works: behold, I have set before you an open door, and no man can shut it: for you have a little strength, and have kept my Word, and have not denied my name. Behold, I will make them of the synagogue of Satan, which say they are Jews, and are not, but do lie; behold, I will make them to come and worship before your feet, and to know that I have Loved you.

Note that Philadelphia had *no* charges against it. It was the only one of the seven for which He publicly stated His love. This means He will return and take back with Him this church, which contains all members of his body. And when that happens, the fifth dispensation, the dispensation of grace, will end, and the dispensation of tribulation, which is the sixth dispensation, will begin. Note the policy of the Enemy: Christ will make those who claim to be the seed of Abraham into the Jews of Satan's synagogue. Why? Satan's falsehood has to imitate the true. Therefore he will set up and control a religious system that resembles the Jewish practice of their religion.

To the church of Symrna, God The Son preaches,

> These things says the first and the last, which was dead and is alive; I know your works, and *tribulation*, and poverty, (but you are rich), and I know the blasphemy of those who say they are Jews, and are not, but *are* the synagogue of Satan. Fear none of those things which you shall suffer: behold, the devil will throw some

of you into prison, that you may be
tested; and you will have tribulation
10 days (ten is humankind's
maximum): be faithful unto death,
and I will give you a crown of life.

He that overcomes, shall not be
hurt of the Second Death.

Smyrna will be the true church of Christ during
the seven years of tribulation. It will suffer
martyrdom through the first years of tribulation
but will triumph just the same, receiving its
crown of life. So we see again, the number three,
which refers to the almighty God, plus the four
added to God the Messiah Savior, equals seven,
which equals God in His church, which results
in God's perfect plan. We have seen the working
of Satan against God's people, the church, and
we will see how he *continues* to work against
God's church, Smyrna, the 144,000 people of
Israel in the seven years of tribulation.

Six

The number six is the number for humankind.
From the record we have a great find in the
generation of Adam: Adam lived for 930 years,

Seth lived for 912 years, Enos lived for 905 years, Cainan lived for 910 years, Mahalaleel lived for 905 years, and Jared lived for 962 years. All of them died, as death is appointed to sinful human beings. According to this rule in the record, which cannot be broken, "as it is appointed unto men once to die, but after this the Judgment." Next we come to the seventh of these men from the generation of Adam, Enoch, about whom we read in the record, "And Enoch walked with God after he begot Methuselah three hundred years and begot sons and daughters: And all the years of Enoch were 365 yrs. And Enoch walked with God; and he was not, for God took him [out of and from earth]" God took him into God's very presence! Enoch did *not* die. How is this possible? All things are possible with God. God shows His power here not in breaking the rule, but in delaying the penalty of death until a specified future time in God's program for the redemption of humankind! Now we know that human beings are of earth, earthy, so humankind's number is six. Six is one short of seven, of course, proving that a human being is just a human being and *not* a god. Also note that Enoch will appear again on planet earth to fulfill his ministry. We will see him later in this book.

The number 666 is presented in the record as a great mystery. For centuries, people have sought to understand it. It has great significance for earth during the end times, from just after the beginning of the sorrows on into the tribulation, which is itself the sixth dispensation. In this future time, there will be a global monetary system that will require the number 666 in order to operate it. Human beings in our time have the technology to use it. In fact, 666 will be a computer-based application to a central computer used in the tribulation to control all money and all transactions on earth. We might ask, how does it work? It is very ingenious. The record tells us how it is going to be put in place, and that will happen sooner than the world thinks. I quote from the word of God:

> Therefore it shall come to pass, that when the Lord has performed his whole work upon mount Zion and Jerusalem, I will punish the stout

heart of the king of Assyria [a type of the Antichrist, and archenemy of Israel], and the glory of his high looks; for he says, by the strength of my hand I have done it, and by my wisdom; for I am prudent: and I have *removed the borders* of the people, and have *robbed their treasures*, and I have put down the inhabitants of the land like a valiant man: And I found as a nest the riches of the people: and as one gathers eggs that are left, I have gathered *all the earth*: and there was none that moved the wing or *objected*. (emphasis added)

How can someone rob the whole earth? The plan is simple.

First, the person must be appointed ruler of planet earth. We know that will happen, as it was prophesied twenty-six hundred years ago. Next, the person must bankrupt every nation on earth by causing each nation to borrow more and more money in order to wastefully spend it on worthless programs and projects. All the nations will know they will *never* be able to *repay* these vast sums.

Second, the person must change the money itself to a new type that can be *controlled by a central bank*.

Finally, the person must outlaw all other forms of money, and replace them (including gold and silver), with "bit dollars." Bits are numbers in computer language. Each bit is arranged to store information of nearly any kind, such as your account number in your local bank. We have been using something like this for years called EFT, which stands for *electronic funds transfer*. EFT allows us to transfer money to another account instead of writing a check or paying with cash. All that needs to be done is simply to require that all currency be exchanged for bit dollars, which really are electronic credits. This will result in the ultimate redistribution of wealth.

The one world government led by this person must confiscate all physical valuables. In exchange, people will gain an account number in the central bank. That account number will *only* be accessible by using the number 666 paired with the personal number assigned to every individual. Further, each personal number will be embedded into an electronic chip that will be inserted into the right hand or forehead of every individual. Individuals will not be able to tattoo the number instead of receiving the chip; it must be *embedded in the flesh*.

This system will accomplish two purposes of the government: the cancellation of all debts and the redistribution of wealth. Everyone with that mark will have an account with the world bank, and those without the mark will have been robbed. The record explains, "And he causes all both *small and great, rich and poor, free and slave,* to receive a mark in their right hand or in their foreheads, and that no one may buy or sell, except one who has the *mark* or the name of the [beastly man], for it is the number of a man: Here is wisdom. Let him who has understanding calculate the number of the [beastly man, which means the Antichrist], for it is the number of a man: His number is 666" (emphasis added). The number can be easily calculated; just change the number from the base ten to the binomial bit zero and one. From the record, we can read further: "Here is wisdom, let him that has wisdom calculate the number of the [Antichrist], his number is 666." Here is the calculation:

666 / 2 = 333
2 x 333 = 666
666 - 666 = 0 (the remainder)

From there, we can calculate as follows:

333 / 2 = 166
2 x 166 = 332
333 - 332 = 1
166 / 2 = 83
2 x 83 = 0
83 - 83=0
83 / 2 = 41
41 x 2 = 82
83 - 82= 1
41 / 2 = 20
20 x 2 = 40
41 - 20 = 1
20 / 2 = 10
10 x 2 = 20
20 - 20 = 0
10 / 2 = 5
2 x 2 = 4
5 – 4 = 1
2 / 2 = 1
1 x 2 = 2
2 -2 = 0
1 / 2 = 0
1 - 0 = 1

When we collect the remainders in a row, we get *0101100101*. This is the number the computer can read, and it equals 666.

The mystery is now understood: 666 will be used as a computer program, and the mark will be a computer chip installed under the skin with a needle. Individuals' account numbers will be read by a scanner, which will be the only way to access bank transactions. In that time period, there will be no other access to wealth. Note that God says, "Anyone with the mark of the [beastly man, antichrist] shall drink of the wine of the wrath of God, which is poured out without mixture, into the cup of his anger; and he shall be tormented with fire and brimstone in the presence of the holy angels and of the Lamb: And the smoke of their torment ascends up for ever and ever: they have no rest day nor night, who worship the [beastly man] and his image, and who ever received the mark of his name." This reminds us of the last gospel that will be preached on earth, and it will be preached by an angel. His message will be, according to the record, "Fear God, and give glory to Him: for the hour of his judgment is here: and worship *Him* that made heaven and earth, and the sea, and the fountains of waters" (emphasis added).

Seven

The number seven is God's special number! Remember, Enoch was number seven in the line of Adam's descent. It speaks of almighty God and His will and work in the lives of human beings. God rested on the seventh day of creation, and sanctified it as a holy day. This day, Sunday, is the first day of our week. Multiples of seven have great significance in the record. The nation Israel was made up of twelve tribes (these tribes were God's special people), but note what happens: Joseph, the eleventh son, married a non-Jewish woman who bore him two sons; these two sons became two new tribes. Therefore, Joseph, whose name means "adding," added two tribes to Israel, bringing the number of tribes from twelve to fourteen.

To explain this mathematically: $14 = 2 \times 7 = (7 + 7) - 12 = 2$. Therefore, there are two distinct flocks of God's sheep. This was God's divine will for Israel, and it continues through the centuries to just before the cross of Christ, where He said, "I have another flock beside this." That flock became His body, the church of the New Testament. Note that 7 x 7 = 49, and on the fiftieth day after, the day of Pentecost, the church was formed.

In the tribulation, there are judgments of seven angels, seven trumpets, seven vials, seven last plagues, and even more instances of this divine number.

We have seen God's perfect number seven, showing us that God is holy and perfect in every way. He is also righteous in every meaning of the word. God is careful to tell us that His plan of redemption for a sinful world is perfect and complete. The eternal record establishes this as follows: "But Christ, because he continues forever, has an unchangeable priesthood. Therefore He is able also to save those to the fullest that come to God by Him; seeing that He always lives to make intercession for them." No one can ever say that God did not do *everything possible to provide salvation for every one who would receive Him*. Now then, that question is settled, there can be nothing left for those who will not receive Him except for judgment.

Resurrection to eternal life comes after the sleep of death for God's redeemed people.

But for those who refuse to accept the truth of God's word, there can be only condemnation after their judgment. The eternal record shows us all the resurrections in God's plan.

Resurrections in God's Plan

There are seven resurrections of God's redeemed people that will occur in different time periods. There is also one more resurrection of several, which actually makes the total eight. God enacts these resurrections according to His will and plan. They are listed in the order of the time period in which they occur.

First, the Lord Jesus Christ rose from the dead three days after His crucified death, never to die again. In His own words, from the eternal record, he says, "I am he that lives and was dead; and, behold, I am alive forevermore, amen; and have the keys of hell and of death."

The second resurrection is described in the record as follows: "And the graves were opened; and many bodies of the saints which slept arose and came out of the graves after Christ's resurrection, and went into the Holy city, and Appeared to many." This event took place very close to the day after He rose from the grave, so that there would be people there who had known Him in their former life on earth. Also, it is recorded that after His resurrection, He was seen by Peter and then by the twelve apostles; after that, He was seen by more than five hundred brethren at once, of whom the larger part remain to this present time: but some of them have passed away, which, for Christians, means they have fallen asleep: "to be absent from this body, is to be Present with the Lord."

The next five resurrections will happen sometime after the present writing of this book.

The third resurrection will occur at the specified time of Jesus' appearance. This will occur in the very near future. It is also for His people only, of both present and past centuries. The record tell us, "So Christ was once offered to bear the sins of many; and to those who look for Him, he will appear the second time apart from sin unto salvation ... For the Lord Himself shall descend from heaven with a shout, with the voice of the archangel, and with the trumpet of God; and the dead in Christ [the sleepers], will rise first: Then we which are alive and remain, shall be caught up together with them in the clouds, to meet the Lord in the air; and so shall we ever be with the Lord." The beginning of the seven-year time of tribulation will coincide with this event.

The fourth resurrection will happen just three-and-a-half years after the beginning of the tribulation, and it will have only two people in it: Enoch and Elijah. According to the record, "The [Antichrist] ... shall make war with them and kill them. And their dead bodies shall lie in the street of the great city where our Lord was crucified ... after three days and a half the Spirit of life from God entered into them, and they stood upon their feet; and great fear fell upon those who saw them. And they heard a great voice from heaven say to them, Come up here. And they ascended up to heaven in a cloud; and their enemies watched them ascend." So we see here that both Enoch and Elijah will return to earth to preach the good news of salvation to a lost world; even in the worst time in the history of this world,

God will make salvation available to *all* who will receive Him. These two prophets were also prophets in the first part of their lives on earth. It has to be these two, because only they can fulfill the eternal Word: "it is appointed to man *once* to die, and after this the judgment" (emphasis added).

The fifth resurrection will occur very near the end of the tribulation. It will consist of those who were saved after the present-day church was called home at the appearance of the Lord Jesus Christ. It will consist of a great multitude of people, according to the record:

> After this I beheld, and lo, a great multitude, which no man could number, of all nations and families, and people, and languages, stood before the throne, and before the Lamb, clothed with white robes, and palms in their hands; And cried with a loud voice saying, 'salvation is of our God who sits upon the throne, and of the Lamb' ... And one of the elders asked me; who are these arrayed in white robes? And where did they come from? And I

said to him, sir you know. And one of the elders answered, saying to me: These are they who came out of Great Tribulation, and have washed their robes, and made them white in the blood of the Lamb.

Therefore: they are before the throne of God, and serve Him day and night in his temple: and he that sits on the throne shall dwell among them.

It is obvious that these are Christians who accepted the Lord, were saved, and then suffered physical death. They have now been resurrected to be with God and to serve Him forever.

The sixth resurrection is a bit different. Six, as you'll remember, is the number of humankind. Six, being one short of seven, reminds humankind that we are *not* God. Even angels have sought to be a god, but that is not possible. There is only one God. The sixth resurrection, then, will be a resurrection of the saints of God who will be saved during the tribulation but who will have lived physically up to the end of it. They will be called "the living"; in the ancient record, we read, "And it shall come to pass, that he that is left in Zion, and he that remains in Jerusalem, shall be called holy, even every one that is written among the Living in Jerusalem." And again the record tells us, "And at that time shall Michael stand up, the great prince who stands for the children [of Israel]; and there shall a time of trouble, such as never was since there was a nation to that time; and then shall they be delivered, every one that shall be found written in the book." That is the book of life.

The seventh resurrection is special. As you'll remember, seven is God's perfect number, so the seventh resurrection is called the foremost resurrection. There will be one thousand years of peace. And the throne of the tabernacle of David, meaning the promised kingdom of David on earth and in heaven, will be inherited, in a physical and literal sense, by the Lord Jesus Christ. He will dwell in its temple on Mount Zion, which will be the capital of earth. As the record states, "And the Angel said to her, Fear not, Mary: for you have found favor with God. And behold, you shall conceive in the womb, and bring forth a son, and shall call his name *Jesus*. He shall be great, and shall be called the Son of the Highest: and the Lord God will give to him the throne of his father David: And he shall reign over the house of Jacob [Israel] for ever; and of *his* kingdom there shall be no end" (emphasis added).

This fulfills the words of our Lord Jesus Christ, which he spoke more than two thousand years ago when He said to Martha, "'I am the resurrection, and the life: and who ever believes in me, though he were dead, yet shall he live: And whoever lives and believes in me shall never die. Do you believe this?' And she said to him, yes Lord: I believe that you are the Christ, the son of God, which should come into the world."

All the people entering the one-thousand-year kingdom will be born again with God's salvation; they will be physical people just like we are. Those born in the this period who receive the Lord Jesus Christ as their savior will *never* die a physical death but will be changed, according to this record: "Now this I say, brethren, that flesh and blood cannot inherit the kingdom of God; neither does corruption inherit incorruption. Behold, I show you a Mystery; we shall not all die [physically], but we shall be changed, in a moment, in the twinkling of an eye, at the last trumpet: for the trumpet shall sound, and the dead shall be raised incorruptible, and we shall be changed. For this corruptible shall put on incorruption, and this mortal must put on immortality." Now this *change* from physical life to *immortal* life [which *defines* resurrection], will be true in the third resurrection thru the seventh resurrection. The words of Jesus Christ, the Lamb of God, will be literally fulfilled.

Eight = a raising of the dead
(no christians are in it).

For number eight, we will examine the eighth resurrection I mentioned above. This is *not*, in fact, an actual resurrection; rather, it is a raising of the dead for judgment. The number eight represents the last and final raising of the remaining dead and unbelieving human beings. They will stand before almighty God, as it is written:

> And I saw a great white throne, and
> him that sat on it, from whose face

the earth and the heaven fled away; and there was no place found for them. And I saw the dead, small and great, stand before God; and the Books were opened: and Another book was opened, which is the Book of Life and the dead were judged out of those things which were written in the books, according to their *works*. And death and hell were cast into the lake of fire. This is the second death. *And whoever was not found written in the Book of Life was cast into the lake of fire.* (emphasis added)

So it is perfectly obvious that where we go after this life upon earth depends on which book our names are written in. Only those who have received the Lord Jesus Christ will be written in His Book of Life. The eternal record states, "Jesus is the true light which lights every man that comes into the world. He was in the world, and the world was made by him, and the world did not know him. He came to his own people [the Jews]; and his own did not receive him. But as many as received him, to them he gave the right and guarantee to become the children of God. To all those who believe on his name."

This is where we all exercise our own God-given power of *choice*. We cannot escape using that choice, for if we refuse to believe on His name, if we have *not* received Him, we will have automatically *prevented* our names from being permanently written in His Book of Life.

God has made it mandatory that everyone *will make the choice*. The right choice is to put our willing belief in the gospel of Christ, which says, "Believe on the Lord Jesus Christ, and you will be saved." At that very moment of belief in receiving Him, our names are *sealed* in the Book of Life. If we refuse to believe, turning away from the Word of God that gives us faith, then we have judged ourselves unworthy of everlasting life.

If the choice of unbelief does not change while we live on this earth, before our physical deaths, then we will have committed the sin unto death, which means the *second death*. The second death is for eternity.

Here is a mystery: Why will humankind refuse this perfect offer of eternal life, made by Jesus Christ on his cross of suffering and death? Number nine is the answer.

Nine

The number nine is the sum of three (which stands for God) and six (which stands for humankind). Adam, the first human being, was created by and for God, not himself. What went wrong? This number has a special application. The addition of three plus six indicates something humankind added over or instead of the true God. It represents humankind's idolatry to a false god and a false religion. Refer to the eternal record: we have this interesting insight into the perversity of sin and its consequences. After Adam sinned and lost his dominion over earth, the influence of Satan in the lives of human beings was unleashed. Through lies and deceit, he meant to draw human beings into his kingdom of darkness. (His kingdom is called Babylon in prophecy.) Satan is at war with God and humankind. He uses humankind in his effort to make himself a god. We see his battlefield in the eternal record, which was written 2,600 years ago and is still in use.

Satan's Battlefield against Humankind in the Commercial System

The king of ancient Babylon had a dream. He did not understand it or even remember it, but it frightened and troubled him greatly. He called in his counselors and demanded they tell him what he had dreamed and what it meant. Of course they had not a clue, so he sentenced them all to death. (Satan has sentenced every human being to death in his personal plan for each of us.) But God is in charge and rules over all the kingdoms of humankind, so our Enemy is limited in his war with us. He can only deceive us into death through the same law that felled Adam; that is, according to the record, "All have sinned and come short of the Glory of God; and; the wages of sin is death; but the gift of God is eternal life thru Jesus Christ our Lord." So our Enemy makes sin seem good to us while making faith in our Lord Jesus Christ seem foolish and undesirable. Our enemy wants us to think: certainly sin is not bad enough to cause death. But here we have the principle of deceit that Satan has used against humankind throughout the ages, namely the lie that good is evil, and evil is good.

The king's dream, the mystery, was revealed by God to His own prophet, who revealed it to all the world in the eternal record of God's Word:

> You O king saw and behold a Great Tall Statue. It was very bright and beautiful to look at, so excellent, and yet in the way a serpent can be beautiful in appearance, but frighting and deadly at the same time. The statue's head was made of pure Gold, his breast and arms of Silver, his belly and thighs of Brass, his legs iron, and his feet part iron and part clay. As you were looking and shivering in fear, you saw a Great stone that was carved from solid rock, without the use of human hands. The rock smashed into the statue's feet of Iron and Clay, and broke them to pieces. Then was the iron, the clay, the brass the silver, and the gold, broken to pieces together, and became like the chaff of the summer threshing floors; and the wind carried them away, that no place was found for them: and the

stone that hit the image became a great mountain, and filled the whole earth.

This is what you dreamed, and we will now show you what it means. You O king, are a king of kings: for the God of heaven has given you a kingdom, power, and strength, and glory. And where ever men dwell, the beasts of the field and the fowls of heaven, he has given into your hand, and has made you ruler over them all. You are this head of gold. And after you, another kingdom shall rise up, inferior to you, and another third kingdom of brass, which shall rule over all the earth. And the fourth kingdom will be strong as Iron: since Iron breaks in pieces, and subdues all things: it shall break them in pieces and bruise them. And you saw the feet and toes, part of Iron and part of miry clay, so this fourth kingdom will be divided; but there will be in it the strength of Iron, and the weakness of clay. The powers of darkness will mingle themselves with the offspring of men: but they shall not stick to one another, even as Iron and clay do not mix. In the days of the 10 toes, which are 10 kings; The God of heaven shall set up a kingdom which will never be destroyed: and it will not be left to other people, but it will break in pieces and consume all these kingdoms, and it will stand forever.

Then the king fell on his face and worshiped the prophet, and said to the prophet; it is true that your God is a God of gods, and a Lord of kings, and he is the one who reveals secrets, seeing that you could do this.

It is most interesting to note that this king, Nebuchadnezzar, knew beyond all doubt that the true God is real and active in the affairs of humankind! And yet, this king, in his later years, introduced a false god and a false religion, which remains in the world to this day.

Nebuchadnezzar made a statue of gold that was sixty cubits tall (one cubit equals one foot nine inches). The height, in our system of measurement, was ninety feet. Ninety is ten times nine; nine, you see, is the number of idolatry, and ten is the number of humankind's limit. The statue was six cubits wide (the number of humankind), and six times 1.75 (one foot nine inches) equals nine feet. So we see how humankind accepted this falsehood totally. The king set this image up in the plain of Dura, in the province of Babylon. Then he sent throughout the kingdom, commanding all government workers (and surely everyone else who was there), at the ceremony of dedication of the image to be god, that at the sound of the trumpet, everyone was to fall down and worship the image. Please note that he ordered all who refused to worship to be executed. This happened 600 BC.

Modern archeologists have confirmed these governments existed in the order and at the dates listed below, beginning approximately 2,600 years ago:

Babylon	Media Persia	Greece	Imperial Rome	Ruled for	Next:
Gold 600 B.C.	Silver 539 B.C.	Brass 336 B.C.	Iron 100 B.C.	Hundreds of Years	We are in the beginning of sorrows, here and now
					The establishment of a global government ruled by the ten toes (kings) of ten commercial regions of earth.

They will appoint the Antichrist—a man of sin, a beastly man—to be the political and religious ruler of the earth. This system will be called by US presidents and other national leaders "The New World Order." Note that this system will be followed exactly as prophesied 2,600 years ago! The ten kings of ten commercial regions of the earth will appoint the beastly man ruler. He then will do the following things:

1. He will immediately begin to consolidate his political support, eliminating all opposition.
2. He will immediately announce himself to be the promised messiah and head of all religions.
3. He will confiscate the money belonging to *all* holders of wealth, both public and private.
4. He will deposit the wealth into his personal account, from which he will redistribute this money as payouts to people. There will be no more poor people and no more rich (except for himself, the ten kings, and whoever else he decides should be rich). No one will

be able to buy or sell without his mark in the person's hand or forehead.

5. He will make a breathing image of himself and will order his false prophet to execute any who do not worship his image.

6. He will set himself up in the temple in Jerusalem, demanding all to worship him as god. Any who refuse will be put to death.

Note that the ancient religion was established with gold (wealth) and enforced with political authority. This is exactly the way it will be done at the proper time as God allows it; God sets the *time*! A writer from the eternal record, addressing Christians of our dispensation, says as follows:"

> Let no one deceive you, for the Day of Christ will not come until many fall away from the truth of God's word; then that man of sin [the Antichrist], shall be revealed, the son of damnation. Who opposes God and exalts himself above all that is called God, or that is worshiped, so that he as if God, sits in the temple

of God, showing himself, claiming to be god: And you know who is suppressing his revealing, that he may be revealed in *God's time*!

For the Mystery of iniquity [lawlessness] is already working: only the one who restrains him will do so until the restrainer is taken out of the way.

And Then shall that Wicked one be revealed, whom the Lord will consume with the spirit of his mouth, and shall destroy with the brightness of his coming: even that wicked one whose coming is after *the working of Satan* with all power and signs and lying wonders. And with all power of deception of unrighteousness in those who perish; because they received not the love of the truth, that they might be saved. And for this cause God shall send them strong delusion, that they should believe a lie: that they might all be damned who did not believe the truth, but had pleasure in unrighteousness. (emphasis added)

But the Antichrist did not count on *climate change*! So this is God's message, especially to we who live in the end times, as prophesied by the prophets.

Ten

The number ten is the base of the most widely used number system in the history of humankind. There are other systems used today. All have their special use, such as the binomial system used in computer applications. But what we see in the use of number ten in the eternal record is God's use of it to send us a message: *humankind has a limit!* The very best people are, after all they have accomplished, still only people, and they cannot exceed their limit, which is indicated by ten in the eternal record and throughout the history of humankind. For example, Jacob said to his wives Rachel and Leah, "I have served your father with all this time, and yet he has, changed my wages 10 times." We note that as we count to ten, we just continue adding the ten at the next interval, on and on, to no stopping place. We have seen how the record says that human beings' most sophisticated political and religious systems, which we will devise when we have the most knowledge and understanding of the sciences, will have seven heads and ten horns. This system plan was revealed to us by God's prophets 2,600 years ago.

Eleven

The number eleven is six plus five. Humankind's number is six, to which God adds his grace, which is five, and that equals eleven. Note that there are seven dispensations (special time periods that God uses to *test* humankind). Surprised? All teachers love to give tests. Why is it this way in the dispensations? From the record, we read, "Having made known to *us* the Mystery of his will, according to his good pleasure which he purposed in himself: That in the dispensation of the fullness of *times*, he will gather together in one all of His redeemed things in Christ, both which are in heaven and which are on earth; even in him" (emphasis added).

These times are all different and have special and distinct sets of conditions that humankind must live under. Here, then, is the test: human beings are sinners, having rejected God. Being in disobedience, they try to replace

God in their own attempt to live forever. This is why human beings love false religions of every kind. Human beings' attempts to be wise enough and good enough to live forever have all failed the test.

God's seven dispensations are as follows:

1. Innocence
Adam, Eve
sinned

2. Conscience
Cain
murdered

3. Human Government
people rejected God

built their own way up

4. Promise
Israel deemed the chosen people
denied their Messiah

5. Grace (we live here)
church
fell away from Christ

6. Tribulation
the natural man
thoughts are evil continually

7. Kingdom of Christ
After one thousand years of peace
made war against God

Each dispensation has a different length of time as determined by God. We know it was thousands of years until the cross of Christ, where the dispensation of grace began and continues. We should take note that humankind fails the test under every environmental and political/religious condition of every dispensation.

Twelve

The number twelve is three times four. As you'll recall, three is the number for God plus the Savior, = 4 which equals Christ, which equals salvation, which equals God's redeemed people, who are separated from the world unto God. From the record, we read, "And Moses said, Thus says the Lord, About midnight I will go out into the midst of Egypt: and all the first born in Egypt shall die, from the firstborn of Pharaoh that sits on his throne, even to the firstborn of the maidservant that is behind the mill; and all the firstborn of beasts. But against any of the firstborn of Israel, a dog shall not move his tongue, against man or beast."

After His death and resurrection, Christ said to His own, "If the world hate you, you know that it hated me before it hated you. If you were *of* the world, the world would love its own: but because you are not of the world, but I have chosen you out of the world; therefore the world hates you. So there is a difference in God's redeemed and those who refuse his salvation. Therefore God's plans for his own are that you may know how that the Lord does put a *difference* between the Egyptians and Israel" (emphasis added). These are the plans that we can understand in our dispensation of time.

To begin, let's go back to the time of the dispensation of promise, when Jacob and his family were living free outside of Egypt. You will recall the story of Joseph and his brothers living in Egypt. The family was captive and away from God, with no evidence of His care for them, yet God heard their prayers and began His program of deliverance. God did this even though they were totally unaware of it until the Lord sent Moses to bring them out. This is a principle of deliverance that has been repeated more than once in the life of Israel. After they came out of Egypt and went into the land promised to their father Abraham, they went astray and into idolatry. So the Lord sent them into captivity to surrounding nations (who hated them). After a while, they repented and turned back to the Lord, and the Lord delivered them. This happened many times up until the rule of David and Solomon, which is when the nation reached its great height of prosperity. But strangely, Israel gradually fell away again, back into sinful ways of living. So the Lord sent them prophet after prophet, with warnings to mend their ways, but they refused; finally He allowed Babylon to destroy Jerusalem and the temple and to carry many captive to Babylon.

Note: When Israel is in captivity, God gives them a year for a day, Numbers 14:34

God gave this captivity a *specific time period*, as follows:

> 70 weeks [of years = 7 x 10 x 7 = 490 years] are determined upon the people Israel and on your holy city, to finish [the penalty] for this transgression, and to make an end of sins, and to make reconciliation for evil, and to bring in everlasting righteousness, and to seal up the

> vision and prophecy, and to anoint the most Holy. Know therefore and understand, that from the going forth to restore and to build Jerusalem until Messiah the prince, shall be [62 + 7 =] 69 weeks [of years], the street shall be again, and the wall, even in troublesome times. After 69 weeks shall Messiah be cut off, but not for himself.

At the crucifixion of Jesus on the cross, Israel's clock *stopped*. After that, in 70 AD, the Roman-occupied city and temple were destroyed. Looking at the math, 7 x 10 tells us this was of God; this era is called the *age* of Israel. Carefully note that the count stopped at 483 years, which is 69 x 7. Therefore, seven years are left to be fulfilled. So Israel is still technically in captivity, away from God, still unaware of the true God and rightful King of Israel, the Lord Jesus Christ. This is proven, even though Israel's people are today in the land of Israel, a sovereign nation. From the eternal record, we read, "and their dead bodies [of Enoch and Elijah] shall lie in the street of the great city, which spiritually is called Sodom and Egypt, where also our Lord was crucified." So we see here that Israel is in *spiritual* captivity because it is apart from the church.

So it is that 490 - 483 = 7 years left of God's plan for the *restoration of Israel*!

The restoration begins with the tribulation dispensation, which is dispensation number six. Let us look again at the record: "For if God did not spare the Natural Branches [Israel], take heed lest he spares not you [the church]. Do not be ignorant of this Mystery ... that blindness in part is happened to Israel until the fullness pf the Gentile [church] has come in: so [beginning with the firstfruits of the harvest] All Israel will be saved: as it is written, there shall come out of Zion [heaven], the Deliverer [Christ], and shall turn away ungodliness from Israel; for this is my covenant unto them, when I shall take away their *sins*."

Now for the firstfruits: The promises to Israel stated above will begin to happen at a point in the future. These great events will take place at the *end* of the dispensation of grace, which is the *beginning* of the seven years left of Israel's age. At the same time, the church, the body of Christ, will be removed from this earth by the return of Jesus Christ, who will take them back with Him. Coinciding with that event, God will cause the firstfruits to physically *see* this wonderful promise fulfilled, which is similar to how the twelve apostles, who were the firstfruits of His church, beheld Him go into heaven. But the apostles remained on earth to start their ministry of fulfilling His command: "All power is given to me in heaven and earth ... go you therefore, and teach all nations to observe all things that I have commanded you."

Twenty-Four

The number twenty-four is two times twelve and six times four, of course. As you'll remember, six is the number of humankind, and four is the number representing the Savior's work, so twenty-four speaks of saved human beings in God's service. We see many examples in the eternal record where God specifically ordered special services to be done by His people. In Israel, during the time after the establishment of the kingship of David, He set up the service groups in courses of twenty-four.

In the priesthood of the tribe of Levi, there were thirty-eight thousand men, thirty years of age and older, chosen for the work as follows: twenty-four thousand were to do the work of the house of the Lord; they served by courses of one thousand in the priesthood. Each course served one half month each year. This was still the order in the days before the Lord Jesus was born. The father of John the Baptist, Zacharias the priest of the course of Abia (who was in the eighth course of the twenty-four), was visited by an angel of the Lord while he was doing his ministry. He was afraid when he saw him, but the angel said, "Fear not; your prayer is heard and your wife Elisabeth shall bear you a son and you will call his name John."

There were twenty-four courses of singers, musicians, porters, and captains of the king's armies. In a future time we will see what the apostle John saw when he was called into the very presence of God in heaven: he saw twenty-four seats round about the throne of God; on them were twenty-four elders, each wearing a golden crown. It is interesting to note that there were twelve tribes of Israel and twelve apostles of the Lord Jesus Christ:

on those twelve men and Himself, He built His church. Twelve Jewish elders plus twelve church elders equals twenty-four elders on thrones in heaven.

One Hundred and Forty-Four Thousand

The number one hundred and forty-four thousand equals the twelve thousand Jews from each of the twelve tribes of Israel. They are the firstfruits of the great harvest (of God's people Israel, from the tribulation of earth). The record states, "Hurt not the earth, neither the sea, nor the trees, till we have sealed the servants of our God in their foreheads, and I heard the number of them which were sealed: A hundred and forty four thousand from all the tribes of Israel." This is a mystery number that has not fully been understood for centuries. If we simply read and follow the record, then one thousand from each tribe times twelve and then times twelve again results in one hundred and forty-four thousand. Being the *firstfruits* (of Israel at the very beginning of the tribulation), these were saved at His appearing in the clouds here above earth and dedicated (sealed) to the service of God and the Lamb.

They preach the gospel of the kingdom to the lost people of earth. They have great success: multitudes turn from sin to salvation but pay with the cost of their physical lives. Yet they go immediately to be with Christ the Lamb and Savior as they stand with Him on heaven's Mount Zion, singing a new song that no one can learn but them.

One Thousand

The number one thousand represents the greatness of God's people; God's people are so great that they are numberless. In the one-thousand-year kingdom of God on earth, a number of people will be produced, and the record tells us that "the number ... is as the sand of the sea."

The one hundred and forty-four thousand will go into a world ruled by the Antichrist, preaching the gospel of the kingdom. During that seven-year period of tribulation, God will call and save the rest of the harvest, Israel, and they will go into the promised kingdom. At the end of the one thousand years of the Messiah's kingdom's reign *on* earth, Satan will be released from his one thousand years of incarceration in the prison of the bottomless pit. He immediately will go into all the world and instigate a rebellion against God. This will happen, because it is possible for people to live in the foremost resurrection under perfect liberty conditions for a normal lifetime and still reject the Lord Jesus Christ as their Savior.

6

The Mystery of Humankind and Climate Change

In Tribulation

Humankind's history is also the history of climate change on the earth. This reality greatly affects life itself. Remember that the earth had to be recreated because Satan sought to destroy it, just as he tries to destroy humankind. When the earth was without form and empty, when it was full of darkness and submersed in water, God intervened and canceled the Destroyer's work by His great power and according to His purpose for humankind, which He loves. So humankind has had solid earth, light, and four seasons; a mist from the ground once watered the plants, which human beings harvested in a perfect climate while living prosperous lives. As time goes by, colossal climate changes take place, as ordered by God. Climate change cannot happen without His direct orders. He establishes them based upon humankind's needs and spiritual condition. Note this example as recorded in the eternal record thousands of years ago.

> And it came to pass, when men began to multiply on the face of the earth, and daughters were born to them, that God's sons [godly men] saw the daughters of men, that they were fair; and they took them wives of their choice. And the Lord said, My spirit shall not always strive with man, he is also flesh, and his days shall be one hundred and twenty years … and God saw that the wickedness of man was great in the earth, and that every imagination of the thoughts of his heart were evil continually. And God said; I am sorry, because I grieve for them and pity them. Therefore, I will *destroy* man from the face of the earth … but Noah found grace in the eyes of the Lord: for he was a just man and upright in this evil environment; and Noah separated himself from their evil ways and walked with God. And God said to Noah, the end of all flesh is come before me; for the

earth is filled with *violence* through them; and, behold I will destroy them *with* the earth. Make you an ark according to my plans which I will show you. (emphasis added)

Soon after in the record, we read,

And the Lord said to Noah, go into the ark, with your family [of seven plus one], for I see you righteous before me in this generation. Of every clean beast, take by sevens, male and female, and beasts that are not clean by two, the male and his female … For after seven days, I will cause it to rain upon the earth forty days and forty nights; and every living substance that I have made I will destroy from off the face of the earth. And Noah did as he was told … And after seven days, the waters of the flood came upon the earth, all the fountains of the of the *great deep* were broken up, and the windows of heaven were opened. And the rain was upon the earth forty days and forty nights. (emphasis added)

This is climate change in gigantic proportions. We see here a principle that connects climate change to judgment:

> And the waters prevailed upon the earth; and the Arc went upon the waters ... and on all the high hills under heaven were covered. Fifteen cubits [over 26 feet] and the mountains were covered, and all the high hills were covered. [It is very interesting to remember that in the "beginning" the earth was submerged.] And all flesh died that moved upon the earth. And every *living substance was destroyed*, which was upon the face of the ground. Only Noah and those with him remained alive, and safe in the ark. God remembered Noah, and made a wind to pass over the earth and the waters receded, so that man could inhabit earth again. (emphasis added)

So humankind was given a second chance to live, and this time people could follow God instead their sinful natures. In their endeavor, they only partially succeeded. For we know there are *many more* catastrophic climate changes to come upon humankind throughout our history! Each one is a *judgment from God*.

Another Mystery Dream

We have seen that Jacob's son Joseph was sold into bondage in the nation of Egypt. Joseph was a man of God. He had the gift of interpreting dreams, a gift that has disappeared in our dispensation, because we walk by faith, not by sight. The Pharaoh, king of Egypt, had a dream that worried him greatly, according to the eternal record, so he called for Joseph and told him the dream:

> And Pharaoh said to him: In my dream, behold, I stood upon the bank of the river: and, saw come up out out of the river, Seven cattle, fat fleshed and well favored; and they fed in a meadow: and then to my surprise, Seven other cows came up after them, poor, ugly and lean fleshed, such as I never saw in Egypt for *badness*. And the lean ugly cows ate up the fat ones: and afterward they were still lean and

ugly, so that I could not tell that they had eaten them. I awoke, then later I saw in my dream, and behold Seven ears of corn came up in one stalk, full and good: and then Seven ears, withered, thin. And blasted with the east wind, sprung up after them: And the thin ears devoured the Seven good ears. I told this to the magicians; but none of them could tell me what it meant.

Then Joseph said to Pharaoh, the dream of Pharaoh is one, and have the same interpretation: for God has shown you what *he is about to do*. The Seven good cows and the Seven good ears are years. And the Seven lean and empty cows that came after them are seven years; and they shall be years of famine. Here is what it means. There will be Seven years of great plenty through all the land of Egypt: And after them shall be seven years of famine; and all the plenty will be forgotten in Egypt, and it will consume the land, for it will be very grievous. Now therefore let Pharaoh find a

man discreet and wise and set him
over the land, to gather up and store
one fifth of the harvest of the good
years to last through the famine,
so that Egypt will not perish.
(emphasis added)

Pharaoh agreed with this interpretation, the
record tells us, and appointed Joseph to the
task described. Then for the first seven years,
Joseph filled the land with corn.

And so it came to pass that the east wind
with no rain came and blasted the land with
climate change. And all the nations came to
Egypt to buy corn because the famine was
harsh in *all lands*. This is how it will be in the
seven-year dispensation of tribulation: great
trouble, suffering, famine, and death upon
earth. There will be no exceptions and no way
to escape that great sorrow.

The Rise of the Antichrist and the Worst Ever Climate Change

We have spoken of the Antichrist, the man
of sin, the beastly man: now it is time for the
details. The eternal record describes him and

what he does in many places. It also tells us the precise conditions of both the political system and the religious one in the days just preceding the tribulation. The Antichrist, as you will recall, even puts both systems together and makes them one.

First let's discuss the political system. We are well aware of the worldwide rise of socialism. This is indicated by *red*, the color of the seven-headed and ten-horned "beastly" government that will soon take rule over earth. Usually socialists' motto has been "equality for the sake of peace." More than one variation of this general *policy* has been used. It was and is very successful in accomplishing its purpose, which is world domination. For example, in France there was a revolution; the masses of the poor rebelled, rising together against a system they blamed for making them poor. So it was a war: the poor against the rich. They slaughtered millions of the royalty, nobles, and others who were successful in trade and other economic endeavors. Their favorite method of execution in 1793 to 1794 was the guillotine, a machine with a heavy sharp blade that lifted high in a rigid frame and then dropped on the neck of the victim. Other nations followed in basically the same fashion. Beheading is being used today by some in the religious world as a means of execution. It will be used during the tribulation, as it is being used now, to murder Christians and others.

Another example is the Russian revolution that took place in 1917, when the communists murdered unnumbered millions. In Germany, the National Socialist Party (called the Nazi party by the world press) and their leader, Hitler, slaughtered millions of innocent people of many nations in their efforts to make Hitler dictator of the world; they had taken control of Germany after World War I. And then there was the Chinese revolution following World War II. It is recorded in the congressional record that the Chinese communists (socialists) slaughtered more than forty million of their own people in order to take power. They got that power, and it is absolute in China today. Many other countries are now socialist in practice, and socialism has already taken over most of the world.

Socialism is not new; it was here when ancient Babel was built thousands of years ago. socialism was the reason God confused their language and made the different races. God's Word makes it very clear that socialism will take over the world, but the form will be just enough different from ancient times and will be called by ever varying names. Its *present* global form is called:

The Ten Toes of Nebuchadnezzar's Dream (Recorded 600 BC)

Nebuchadnezzar's dream featured a lion with ten horns and iron teeth, plus an additional little horn. The dream also had a great red dragon, Satan himself, with seven heads, seven crowns, and ten horns. Then there was a beast that came out of the Mediterranean Sea; the beast had seven heads and ten horns with ten crowns on them.

This beast symbolizes the government of Satan through his Antichrist, whose ancestry will be Mediterranean. His government will be structured exactly as prophesied, with seven heads and ten horns and carrying a woman who is arrayed in purple, scarlet, gold, and precious stones. On her forehead will be written this title: *Mystery Babylon the Great, the Mother of Harlots and Abominations of Earth.*

We must remember that Satan works constantly in the affairs of human beings. Mystery Babylon is a system that he has devised that consists of two parts combined as one:

> (1) The System of the Globally Corrupt Commercial and Political Beast (the Antichrist)

> (2) The System of the Global Woman of Religious Occult Satan Worship (who also steals and murders, and who rides the beast)

Both of these systems are striving to be *ruler of the world*. How can this be?

A statement made by a former Russian premier is revealing: "We cannot have a new world order without religion." A former president of a notorious supporter of terrorists said, "Islam and Mohamed is the answers to modern man's need; world nations will accept Islam, if they could have it with Islam's conditions." They will be successful in setting the system up just as described. For the religious section, I quote the record: "The [beastly man] had a mouth like a lion, and Satan gave him his power and his throne, and great authority. And I saw one of his heads as it were wounded to death, and his deadly wound was healed: and They worshiped Satan, which gave power to the beast, and they worshiped the beast; saying: Who is like the beast, who is able to make war with him?"

The answer to the mystery of the woman and the beast she rides is right in front of our noses. It should be of interest to note the US dollar bill's inscription on the banner at the bottom of the pyramid: *"novus ordo seclorum."* Many presidents, statesmen, and world leaders have publicly called it "the new world order." When this system is completely set up, the Antichrist, the little horn, will take all political *and* military control of planet earth. Even as long ago as the 1960s, the then US president made the statement publicly that "National sovereignty is *outdated*" (emphasis added). It is here now but being *restrained* from completion by God until He is ready for it to be revealed. Following are the details of the events that will happen when the new world order takes power.

First, the Antichrist will appear riding a white horse; he will be imitating the coming of the true Messiah. He will have a bow and a crown that was given to him, and he will go forth conquering and to conquer. This indicates something of great importance: he will not be revealed until he is *given* a crown. This crown will be a crown of one of the heads but will not (at first) rule over the ten kings yet. In order to rule the globe, he will have to grab power by political and fraudulent means. This scenario is prophesied in the record:

> And when the transgressors have come to full wickedness, a king of strong impudent countenance shall take office; and his power will be mighty, but not of himself: and he shall destroy remarkably, and shall successfully continue that practice, even destroying the mighty and holy people. And thru his policy he will cause fraud and deceit to prosper in his hand; and he shall magnify himself in his heart, and by peace

[and in the name of peace] shall destroy many: he also shall stand up against the Prince of princes [Christ Himself], but he shall be broken, but not with human hands.

It seems incredible that peace can be made to destroy, but we see this in the record; for example, consider the mystery of the seven seals, which only Christ can open, and the mystery of the four horseman of the Apocalypse, which will come out when the seals are opened and which will reveal events that will happen during the seven years of the tribulation. With the first seal and first horse, the record says we will see the Antichrist on the white horse, [white means he is imitatiting the righteous power of the true Messiah] conquering. The next seal will show a red horse, which stands for war. The horse will go out, and to the rider will be given the power to take peace from the whole earth. Because they will need to kill one another, a great sword will be given to him. So the so-called "peace" will not last long. With the third seal, there will be a black horse, which stands for famine, and the rider will have a pair of scales in his hand. He will have two measuring devises in his hand, suggesting two standards of distributing food and energy to the people. The voice of the record reports, "And I heard a voice saying, 'A measure of wheat for a penny, and three measures of barley, for a penny, and do not injure the oil and the wine.'" The oil and wine and choice foods that go with them are for the rich, so there will surely be two standards of food distribution to the people.

Government control of *all* food sources will be a result of the destruction of humankind and the destruction of the earth. The economy is currently being destroyed, and food production is currently greatly reduced; there are not enough workers producing at full capacity to catch up to the need. More than half of US citizens do *not work*. Socialism discourages work, giving free wealth to the non-producers from taxpayers who cannot possibly supply the need.

The result is famine, which comes very quickly and causes many to die. The record says, "And I looked and behold, a Pale Horse: and his name that sat upon him was Death, and Hell followed with him. And power was given them [the 4 Riders] over the fourth part of the earth to kill with sword, and with hunger, and with death, and with the beasts of the earth."

These things are happening not because humankind wanted it but because there is a law that cannot be broken: whatever we sow, so shall we also reap. Horrible as it is, that is only the beginning of a righteous God's judgments upon earth. From now on, climate change will come with increasing destruction on earth.

The fifth seal will show the power of religious hatred exercised by the followers of the false god, the Antichrist, and his subjects. The eternal record explains,

> And when he had opened the Fifth Seal, I saw under the alter the souls of those who were slain for the Word of God, and for the Testimony which they held: and the cried with a loud voice, saying, How long, O Lord, holy and true, do you not avenge our blood on them that dwell on the earth? And white robes were given to every one of them; and it was said to them, that they should rest for a little while, until their fellow

servants and also their brethren that
should be killed as they were, should
be fulfilled.

The sixth seal will open next. Remember the number of humankind (six) and the human fear of climate change? Climate change will continue to come upon human beings from the hand of God, and we will be powerless to do anything about it. The eternal record describes the events following the opening of the sixth seal: "And I beheld when he opened the sixth seal, and there was a Great Earthquake; and the sun became black as sackcloth of hair, and the Moon became as blood; and the stars fell to the earth, even as a fig casts off its untimely fruit, when it is shaken of a mighty wind [but there is much more] to come. And the heaven [atmosphere] departed as a scroll when it is rolled together; and every mountain and island were moved out of their places." How is this *great climate change* possible?

The seventh seal will be the next to open. The record describes the event as follows:

> And when he had opened the
> Seventh Seal, there was silence in

in heaven for about a half hour …
and I saw seven angels standing
before God, and they were given
seven trumpets, and another angel
came and stood at the alter, with a
golden censer that he should offer
incense along with the prayers of all
God's people; upon the golden alter
before the throne. And the smoke
of the incense came up before God
along with the prayers of his people.
And the angel took the censer and
filled it with fire from the altar, and
cast it into the earth: and there were
voices and thunders, and lightning,
and an earthquake.

Then the angels with the seven
trumpets prepared to sound. The
first sounded and there fell hail and
fire mixed with blood, and they
were cast upon the earth: and one
third of the trees were burnt up,
and all green grass was burnt up.
[This indicates God's response to
the prayers of His people. They were
and are persecuted without cause by
those intolerant haters of Christian
religious freedom.]

And the second angel sounded, and as it were a great mountain burning with fire was cast into the sea: and third part of the sea became blood, and one third of the living creatures that were in the sea died; and one third of the ships were destroyed. And the third angel sounded and a great star fell from heaven, burning as if it were a lamp, and it fell upon one third of the rivers, and upon the fountains of waters; And the name of the star is called wormwood [bitter, calamity]; and many died of the waters because they were poison. And the fourth angel sounded, and the third part of the sun was smitten [hit with great force], and the third part of the moon, and stars; so that a third of them were darkened and did not shine for a third of the day.

It is most interesting that the third, three, is the number of the Father, Son, and Holy Spirit.

Now there is global climate change, but it cannot be blamed on people. In fact, it's just the opposite: God is making people pay for hating Him and rejecting His Son who died on the cross to provide free salvation to all who will receive Him. This is predetermined by God, and it will come to pass just as He told us it would twenty-six hundred years ago. Isaiah the prophet recorded this prophecy in the eternal record: "For behold the *day of the Lord*, is coming, cruel both with wrath and fierce anger, to lay the land desolate: and he shall destroy the Sinners Out of It! For the stars of heaven and its constellations; shall not give their light: the sun shall be darkened in it's going forth, and the moon will not cause it's light to shine. And *I will punish the world for their evil, and the wicked for their iniquity; and I will cause the arrogancy of the proud to cease, and I will lay low the haughtiness of the terrible*" (emphasis added). There is much more climate change to follow: "I will make a man more scarce than fine gold; even more than the golden wedge of Ophir (because his numbers on earth are rapidly dwindling). Therefore I will shake the heavens, and the earth shall move *out of her place*, in the wrath of the Lord of hosts, and in the day of his fierce anger" (emphasis added).

Imagine the changes in earth's climate that will occur when this planet is *out of orbit*! The same prophet adds these details in another place in the record:

> Fear, and the pit, and the snare, are upon you O *inhabitant* of the earth. And it shall come to pass, that he that is fleeing from the noise of the fear shall fall into the pit; and he that comes up out of the pit shall be taken in the snare: for the windows from on high are open, and the foundations of the earth shake. The earth is utterly broken down, the earth is clean dissolved, the earth is moved exceedingly. The earth shall reel back and forth like a drunkard, and shall be removed like a cottage; and the transgression of it shall be heavy upon it; and it shall fall and not rise again. And it will come to pass in that day, that the Lord shall punish the host of the *high ones* that are on high [Remember those followers of Satan in the heavenly places?] *and* the kings of the earth upon earth.

> And they shall be gathered together,
> as prisoners are gathered in the pit,
> and shall be shut up in the prison,
> and after many days they shall be
> visited. (emphasis added)

Note that the punishment of those in the preceding passage is given in more detail. This should be of great interest to everyone of our day when we remember the terrorist attacks of the past few years and the wars against so-called "terror." Many of the nations that practiced terror wars are actually named in the eternal record of humankind. These nations "caused" the terror. Consider this message from God written more that twenty-five hundred years ago and recorded by the prophet Ezekiel as follows:

> The strong among the mighty shall
> speak out of the midst of ... *hell* ...
> they are gone down there, they lie
> uncircumcised, slain by the sword.
> Syria is there and all his company:
> his graves are about him all of them
> slain by the sword: Whose graves are
> set in the sides of the pit, and their

company, all of them slain, fallen by the sword, which *caused terror* in the land of the living. Elam [Iran], is there, with all of his multitude, slain by the sword, gone down uncircumcised into the lower parts of the earth, which *caused their terror* in the land of the living. (emphasis added)

Egypt and other lands are also named among those that suffer this fate. God is showing the unbreakable law that what you sow, you will reap: "Thus says the Lord God, for I have *caused* my *terror in the land of the living*" (emphasis added). (This terror is still awaiting us in future, but God speaks as if it is already done).

Here is an account listing some of God's terror, which He will pour out at the proper time for what will happen to Israel during the middle of the tribulation:

Therefore son of man, prophesy and say to Gog, thus says the Lord God; in that day when my people of Israel dwell safely, shall you not know it? And you will come from your place

out of the north parts, you and many
people with you, all of them riding
upon horses, a great company, and
a mighty army: and you shall come
up against my people Israel, as a
Cloud to cover the land; it shall be
in the latter days, and *I will bring you*
against *my land*, that they who do not
believe in me; may *know me*, when
I shall be revered in you, O Gog,
before their eyes.

Thus says the Lord God; are you
the one of whom I have spoken in
old time by my servants the prophets
of Israel, which prophesied in those
days, that I would bring you against
them? And it shall happen that,
when Gog shall come against the
land of Israel, says the Lord God,
that my fierce anger shall come up
in my face, for in my jealousy and in
the fire of my wrath I have spoken,
Surely in that day there will be a
great shaking in the land of Israel;
so that the fish of the sea, and the
fowls of the heaven, and the beasts
of the field, and all creeping things
upon the earth, and all the people

on earth, shall *shake at my presence*;
and the mountains shall fall down,
the steep places will fall, and every
wall shall fall to the ground. And
I will call for a sword against Gog
throughout all my mountains, says
the Lord God: every man's sword
shall be against his brother. And I
will plead against him with *pestilence
and with blood; and I will rain upon him
and on his bands, and upon the many
people with him, an over flowing rain,
and great hailstones, fire and brimstone.*
Thus will I magnify and hallow
myself; and I will be known in the
eyes of many nations, and they shall
know that I am the Lord. (emphasis
added)

In this terror from the Lord, we also note the
huge climate change coming down from God
that pollutes the atmosphere and the soil. This
is what we expect, as the accounts of climate
change continue:

And the fifth angel sounded, and I
saw a star fall from heaven to earth:
and to him was given the key of the

bottomless pit. And a smoke rose out of the pit, as the smoke of a great furnace; and the sun and the air were darkened by it [more climate change], and locusts came out of the smoke to the earth; and to them was given power, as scorpions of the earth have power. And they were commanded not to hurt green grass, trees or any green plant; but only those men which do not have the seal of God in their foreheads. And they were told to Not kill men, but that they should torment them for five months: and their torment was like a scorpion when he stings someone. In those days men shall seek death, and shall not find it; and shall desire to die, but they cannot bring about their death. (emphasis added)

It should be of interest to note that in recent newscasts, more than a dozen people have been reported to have died from the stings of large hornets, some over three inches in length. Many others have been wounded. The eternal record continues:

And the sixth angel sounded: I heard a voice from the four horns of the golden altar which is before God, saying to the angel; "Loose the four angels which are bound in the great river Euphrates." And they were loosed to slay the third part of men. And the number of the army was two hundred million.

The army had breast plates if fire and brimstone, rode horses which had heads like lions, and fire, smoke and brimstone issued from their mouths. One third of men were killed by these. And the rest of the men which were not killed by them; did not repent nor turn from their murders, or use of illegal drugs, or of their fornication, or of their thefts.

Climate Change Expanded

The eternal record of humankind further illuminates the prophecies regarding climate change:

And a voice from the temple said to the seven angels, go your ways and pour out the 7 Vials of the wrath of God upon the earth. The first Vial was poured out on the earth; and there fell a injurious and painful sore upon the people who had the mark of the Antichrist, and those who worshiped his image. And the second Vial was poured out on the sea; and it became as the blood of a dead man: and every living soul in the sea died.

The third Vial was poured out upon the rivers, and fountains of waters; and they became blood. And I heard the angel of the waters say, You are righteous O Lord, which are, and were, and shall be, because you have judged thus. For they have shed the blood of saints and prophets, and you have given them blood to drink; for they are worthy of it. And I heard another out of the alter say; Even so Lord God Almighty, true and righteous are your judgments.

Then the fourth angel poured out his Vial upon the sun; and power was given to him to scorch men with fire. And they were scorched

with great heat, and blasphemed
the name of God, who has power
over these plagues: and they did not
repent to give him glory.

I must assume that most people have known
for a long time about the (so-called) global
warming problem facing humankind, so they
say we must pay a global tax to protect us
from climate change. They say that *we* must
protect Mother Earth. Such reasoning does
not take into account the fact that humankind
is *powerless* to prevent any climate change and
global warming! No matter how powerful the
politicians are, they do not control the sun
and stars of the universe. The greatest climate
change the earth has seen or will see in the
future has *already been scheduled*, to the very
minute, by almighty God. The *mystery* is that
humankind was warned about it two thousand
years ago by the one who holds *all* power in
existence. These words were spoken by the
Christ of Calvary.

This is not the worst of, nor the end of,
judgments on humankind in general, but
the eternal record continues to report on the

prophecy, now directed toward the Antichrist, the Enemy of God and humankind: "The fifth angel poured out his Vial upon the throne of the antichrist; and his kingdom was full of darkness; and they gnawed their tongues for pain, and blasphemed the God of heaven because of their pains and sores, and repented not of their deeds." This tells us the nature of sin. It is so terrible that human beings could not reason beyond the lies of Satan, who deceived the whole world into the worship of Satan himself and of his false messiah.

The record continues as follows:

> The sixth angel poured his Vial on the great river Euphrates; and the water of it was dried up to prepare the way of the kings of the east. [Now the ten kings have decided to invade and conquer what is left of earth.] I saw three unclean spirits come out of the mouth of Satan and the mouth of the antichrist, and out of the mouth of the false prophet. For they are the spirits of devils, working miracles. And they go out to the kings of the earth and of the

whole world, to gather them together
to the battle of that great day of God
Almighty.

Now we know what all this is really about:
war between the *evil* powers of darkness and
almighty God. The record continues:

> And he gathered them together
> into a place in the Hebrew tongue
> called Armageddon. And the
> seventh poured his vial into the
> air; and there came a great voice
> out of the temple of heaven, from
> the throne, saying, It is done. And
> there were voices, and thunders,
> and lightnings; and there was a
> great earthquake, such as had not
> happened since men were on the
> earth, so powerful and so great.
> And the great city was divided into
> three parts, and the cities of the
> nations fell: and *great Babylon* came
> into remembrance before God, to
> give her the cup of the wine of the
> fierceness of his wrath. (emphasis
> added)

I can now give the details of the great climate change and of the destruction of the commercial system of planet earth. As the record states, the following announcement was made from heaven: "Babylon the great is fallen, is fallen, and is become the habitation of devils, and the hold of every foul spirit, and a cage of every unclean and hateful bird. For All Nations have drunk of the wine of the wrath of her fornication, And the kings of earth have committed fornication with her, and the merchants of the earth are made rich through the abundance of her delicacies." Note there are two beneficiaries of this system: First, the politicians (kings) literally sold out their people for personal wealth of every kind available within the system. They robbed their people for personal gain and power within the system. Second, the merchants profited greatly from a monopolistic market, where they could control the price of everything sold on earth. They could set any price they chose, because the entire system was the one and only market. It might as well be called the money rule.

Here is God's description of great Babylon, personified as a woman: "Come out of her my people, so you will not partake of her sins, and that you not receive of her plagues. For her sins have reached to heaven, and God has remembered her iniquities [lawlessness]." There is a struggle within the system for dominance; who wins is nobody's choice except for God's; God makes the choice that best suits His purpose, for even in this terrible world, God still is saving and delivering His own people. The *beast* the woman is riding is the system designed and sustained by Satan. We have seen this system before; but now more details are revealed as to its nature and purpose. "The ten horns" of the (commercial, military, idolatrous, and satanic) system have a plan in mind, according to the record: "The ten horns are ten kings, who have received no kingdom as yet; but receive power for 7 years with the antichrist. These have one mind, and shall give their power and strength to the antichrist."

The record continues to describe the ten horns/kings as follows:

> They will make war with the Lamb.
> And the Lamb shall overcome them:
> for He is Lord of lords, and King of

kings: and they that are with him are called, and chosen, and faithful. And he said to me, the waters you saw where the Harlot sits, are peoples, multitudes, and languages. And the ten horns shall hate the Harlot, and shall make her desolate and naked, and shall eat her flesh, and burn her with fire. For God has put in their hearts to fulfill his will, and to agree to give their kingdom to the antichrist, until the words of God shall be fulfilled. And the woman you saw is that great city [the future commercial capital of earth], which rules over the kings of the earth.

Note first that after the Antichrist will receive power from Satan, he will go out to make war and conquer. Second, we know that Satan and his angels made war in heaven against God and were thrown out of heaven as a result. Third, the massive anti-Jewish coalition will continue to war against Israel, and God will destroy them. Fourth, the ten kings will make war with the Lamb, and will be overcome. Next will come the people's battle of Armageddon.

Then there will be a battle against Jerusalem, as prophesied in the record:

> The word of the Lord for Israel ... behold I will make Jerusalem a cup of trembling to all the people around about them, when they shall be in the siege both against Judah and Jerusalem. And in that day I will make Jerusalem a burdensome stone for all people: all that burden themselves with it shall be cut in pieces, though *all* the people of the earth shall be Gathered Together against it ... In all the land of Israel, two thirds of the people will be cut off and die, but the one third that's left; I will bring through the fire, and will refine them as silver is refined, and I will test them as gold is tested: they will call upon my name, and I will hear them: and I will say, it is my people: and they will say, The Lord is my God.
>
> All these nations will come against Jerusalem in battle; and the city shall be taken, and the houses plundered and the women raped;

and half of the city shall be captured:
but what's left of the people will not
be taken from the city. Then The
Lord will go forth and fight against
those nations, as when he fought in
the day of battle.

Now we will see the results of this great battle,
as we are told what happens to the enemies of
God. The record prophesies as follows:

He now shows his Almighty power
as the King over all the earth, in
that day his name will be one. He
will hit them with a plague against
all those fighting against Jerusalem:
their flesh shall consume away while
they stand on their feet, and their
eyes shall consume away in their
sockets, and their tongues shall
consume away in their mouths.
And the Lord will send confusion
among them, and everyone will fight
against his comrade; and Judah will
fight at Jerusalem; And the wealth
of all nations round about will be
gathered together, gold, silver, and
apparel, in great abundance.

Note that there is no mention of "bit" money.

Prophets of both the Old and New Testaments confirm the great appearance of God in this battle. Now we will look at the last account of this battle, written in the eternal word of God by the apostle John. The destruction that strikes humankind in these events also brings great climate change in the earth, so that humankind's habitation will never be the same. John's writings reveal a *promise* for which humankind has been looking for thousands of years. This explains the deepest mysteries, almost never even spoken of to the peoples of earth. Here is a quotation from the last book of the eternal record of humankind:

> And I saw heaven opened, and behold a white horse; and he that sat upon him is called faithful and true, and in righteousness he does judge and make war. His eyes were as a flame of fire, and on his head were many crowns; and he had a name written that no man knew but himself. And he was clothed with a garment dipped in blood:

and his name is called The Word of God. And the armies which were in heaven followed him on white horses, clothed in fine linen, white and clean. And out of his mouth goes a sharp Two Edged Sword, that with it he should strike the nations: and he shall rule them with a rod of iron: and he treads the wine press of the fierceness and wrath of Almighty God. And he had on his garment and on his thigh a name written, KING OF KINGS, AND LORD OF LORDS.

And I saw an angel standing in the sun; and he cried with a loud voice, saying to all the fowls that fly in the heavens, come and gather yourselves to the supper of the great God. That you may eat the flesh of kings, and of captains, and mighty men, and the flesh of horses and those that set on them, and the flesh of all men, both free and slave, both small and great. And I saw the antichrist, and the kings of the earth, and their armies, gathered together to make war against him that sat on the horse, and against his army. And the antichrist was arrested, and with him the false prophet that performed miracles before him, with which he deceived those who had received the *mark* of the antichrist, and those who had worshiped his image. These were both cast alive into a lake of fire burning with brimstone. And those left were slain with the sword of him that sat upon the horse, which sword proceeded out of his mouth; and all the fowls were *filled with their flesh*. (emphasis added).

This great King of Kings and Lord of Lords is the very one who came to earth as the babe in the manger, who grew to be the Son of Man; He is the Good Shepherd, the Lamb of God, the *crucified* Christ of the cross, and the *first to be born from the dead*. His promises made over two thousand years ago are and will be fulfilled just as He said then: "For as the lightning comes out of the east, and shines even to the west; so shall the coming of the Son of man be. For wherever the carcass is, there will the eagles be gathered together." His words also say,

> Immediately after those days of Tribulation, the sun will be darkened, and the moon will not give its light, and the stars shall fall from heaven, and the powers of the heaven will be shaken: and *then* shall the sign of the Son of man appear in heaven: and then all the tribes of the earth shall *mourn*, and they shall see the Son of man coming in the clouds of heaven with power and great glory. And he will send his angels with a great sound of a trumpet, and they will *gather* together his elect from the four winds, from one end of heaven to the other. (emphasis added)

Who are these elect?

The *elect* are the Jewish people first, followed by the rest of the nations who were saved during the seven years of tribulation and survived in their *mortal* bodies until the very end. They will finally rest from their labors (of survival) and will then be a part of the one thousand years of peace of the kingdom of David that follows. Absolutely *no* unsaved will go in to defile His kingdom's holiness. The Devil that deceived the world will be locked up in the bottomless pit for one thousand years. The *law of the world* will be the Ten Commandments of God. Now this will be the perfect environment and *climate* for humankind. The Ten Commandments of God and the Word of God is also called the Perfect Law of Liberty.

7

Jesus Christ, the Perfect Man, Rules His Perfect Kingdom with His Totally Redeemed Humankind in a Perfect, Unchangeable Climate

We can read about the ultimate climate change in the eternal record of humankind, the Holy Bible:

> And he brought me to the door of the Temple; and behold, waters issued out from under the threshold of the Temple eastward: for the forefront of the Temple was toward the east, and the waters came down from the right side of it, at the south side of the alter. Then he brought me out by the way of the gate northward, and led me outside toward the gate that faces east; and behold, waters ran out on the right side. And when the man with a measuring line in his hand went east, he measured a thousand

cubits, and he caused me to pass
through the waters: the waters were
to the ankles. And he measured a
thousand more, and he caused me to
pass through them and they were to
the knees. And he measured another
thousand, and caused me to pass
through, and they were to the loins.
And he measured a thousand: it was
a river that I could not pass through,
for the waters were risen, waters to
swim in, a river that could not be
passed through.

And he said to me; son of man
have you seen this? And he led me
and brought me back to the bank of
the river. When I returned, I saw
on the bank of the river, there were
very many trees on both sides. And
he said to me, these waters issue out
to the east country, and go down to
the Desert, and go into the sea: and
when they go into the sea, the waters
will be healed. And then, wherever
the river goes every thing will live,
and there shall be a great multitude
of fish. And the fishermen will stand
upon it, and there will be a place

from Engedi even to En-eglaim; where they spread their nets. Their fish will be according to their kinds, as the fish of the great sea, exceeding many. But the river's marshes and its pools will not be healed; they shall be given to salt.

And on both sides of the river bank, shall grow all trees for meat, whose leaves shall not fade, neither will their fruit fail: it will bring forth new fruit every month, for its waters issue out of the sanctuary, and the fruit shall be for food, and the leaves for medicine.

Elsewhere the record documents as follows:

And the parched ground shall become a pool, and the thirsty land, will have springs of water: in the habitations of serpents, where each lay, shall be grass with reeds and papyrus. And a highway shall be there, and a Way, which shall be called the way of holiness; the unclean shall not pass over it; but it shall be for those: the wayfaring men, though fools, shall not err therein. No lion will be there, nor any ravenous beast will be on it, there will be none there; but the redeemed shall walk there. And the ransomed of the Lord shall return, and come to Zion with songs and everlasting joy upon their heads: they shall obtain joy and gladness, and sorrow and sighing will flee away.

In yet another section of this holy record, the Bible, we read,

And there shall come forth a rod out of the stem of Jesse, and a branch shall grow out of his roots ... and the spirit of the Lord shall rest upon him ... and shall make him of quick understanding in the fear of the Lord; and he shall not judge after the sight of his eyes, neither reprove after the hearing of his ears: but with righteousness shall he judge the poor, and reprove with equity for the meek of the earth; and he will smite the earth with the rod of his mouth, and with the breath of his lips he will slay the wicked. And righteousness shall be the girdle of his loins, and faithfulness the girdle of his strength. The wolf also will dwell with the lamb, and the leopard shall lie down with the kid; and the calf and the young lion together; and a little child shall lead them. And the cow and the bear shall feed; there, and their young ones will lie down together: and the lion shall eat straw like the ox … they will not hurt nor destroy in all my holy kingdom: for the earth shall be full of the knowledge of the Lord, as waters that cover the sea.

And it shall come to pass in that day, that the Lord shall set his hand again the second time to recover the remnant of his people which shall be left from Syria, and from Egypt, from Pathros, and from Iran, from Iraq, and from Hamath, and from the Islands of the sea. And he shall set up a banner to the nations, and shall assemble the outcasts of Israel, and gather together the dispersed of Judah from the four corners of the earth.

These things can only happen in the one thousand years of peace, the kingdom of our Lord Jesus Christ. The record says, "But he chose the tribe of Judah, the mount Zion that he loved," and we will see Him again standing on Mount Zion, in heaven, with the 144,000 firstfruits of Israel from the tribulation. He will rule His people and all others on the earth. He is the Lion of the tribe of Judah and Lord of Lords and King of Kings, and He will defeat the ten kings in the war they make against Him in heaven. At His return to earth, He will continue to wear the name and title of absolute unquestioned rule: King of Kings and Lord of Lords.

The kingdom and reign of the great King will be the only one that will have ever been *righteous* in all the history of humankind, past, present, and future. The record says, "And it shall come to pass in the last days, that the government of the Lord's house shall be established above all other governments, and it will be exalted above all of them. And many shall go and say, Come and let us go up to the mountain of the Lord, to the house of the God of Jacob; and he will teach his ways, and we will walk in his paths; for out of Zion the *law* will go forth, and the Word of the Lord from Jerusalem" (emphasis added).

The kingdom of God on earth will certainly not be a Mystery, for as predicted in ancient times, "The seventh year shall be a sabbath of rest to the *land*" (emphasis added). Now earth gets rest from the ravages of wars, pollution, and the destruction of humankind. A new policy of peace and blessing awaits us, according to the eternal record: "the natural growth coming from the earth during the 50th sabbath of the land shall be for your food, and for your animals. And you shall number seven Sabbaths of years, forty nine years, and the fiftieth year shall be hallowed, and you shall blow the trumpet, and proclaim *liberty* throughout all the land to all the inhabitants of the earth. It shall be a Jubilee to you" (emphasis added). This is the sound of a joyful festival of rest and peace for all.

Now we can and will rejoice in the marvelous blessing of God. Let us remember the translation of Enoch, so it is our experience: "God has delivered *us* from the power of darkness, and has Translated us into the

Kingdom of his dear Son" (emphasis added). Where then is the mystery? It is explained this way: "For you are worthy to take the book and open its seals; for you were slain and have redeemed us to God by your blood out of every kindred, language, people and nation; and have made us to our God and Christ, kings and priests: and we shall reign *with him* a thousand years" (emphasis added).

The translation of God's people has been spoken of for thousands of years. Now we will see the reality of it in the kingdom of our Lord Jesus Christ when David's greater Son reigns from Mount Zion in Jerusalem. The key of David will be used to open His kingdom on earth.

8

The Mystery of Humankind's Complete Failure

We have seen the failure of humankind in every *different* dispensation. There has to be proof of the sinfulness of sin. Humankind has tried and tried throughout the centuries to overcome and conquer sin and death without success. Every condition of humankind's environment has been tried except one: the perfect kingdom of God upon earth. To begin with, *none* of the sinners of all of history will be allowed to go into that new kingdom on earth. So, humankind will get a new start. Three groups will go into that one thousand years of perfection: first, the redeemed people of Israel and Jewish heritage in their natural bodies will go. Second, the redeemed of all other nations who were saved during the tribulation will go. Third, there will be all the redeemed of all ages, in their glorified incorruptible bodies. They will say, having received the following promise from the Bible: "the Church, the body of Christ: You have made us kings and priests, and *we* shall reign on the earth" (emphasis added).

The new translated saints will be in prime condition. The one thousand years will be the foremost resurrection, which means that those who live then and who will be saved in the tribulation will *never* die. Similarly, those living people who were taken up at Christ's return did not die but were changed instantly into the eternal glorious beings God meant for us to be. To make sure to remove all temptation, God will put the Enemy of humankind, the Devil, into prison for a one thousand years. For the first time ever, humankind will be totally on its own!

The natural children born in that time will be born *un*redeemed, even if their parents are Christians. Therefore, there will be a condition of redeemed beings (in the natural flesh) living with their *un*redeemed children of the natural flesh. Strange as it may seem, this condition will exist and will continue right up to the end of the thousand years. We can see that these will need to be saved during the kingdom time. The record says,

Be you glad and rejoice forever in that which I create: for; behold I create Jerusalem a rejoicing, and her people a joy. And I will rejoice in Jerusalem, and joy in my people: and the voice of weeping shall be no more heard in her, nor the voice of crying.

There will be no one there an infant of days, nor and old man that has not fulfilled his days: for the child shall die a hundred years old; but the sinner being a hundred years old shall be accursed.

And they shall build houses and inhabit them; and they shall plant vineyards, and eat the fruit of them. They shall not build and another inhabit; they shall not plant and another eat: as the days of a tree are the days of my people, and my *elect* shall long enjoy the work of their hands; they shall not labor in vain, nor bring forth for trouble; for they are the seed of the blessed of the Lord, and their offspring with them.

And it will come to pass, that before they call, I will answer; and while they are yet speaking, I will hear. The wolf and the lamb shall feed together, and the lion shall eat straw like the bullock: and dust shall be the serpent's meat. They shall not hurt nor destroy in all my holy mountain says the Lord. (emphasis added)

What a tremendously wonderful place to be in. Yet even this perfect place cannot take sin from humankind; we must realize that only the Lord Jesus Christ Himself is able to wash us from our sins by His blood. We remember what the record says:

For when we were in the flesh, the motions of sins as defined by the law, worked in our members to bring forth fruit to our death. But now We are delivered from the law, that being dead in where we were held; we should serve in newness of the spirit, and not in the oldness of the letter … for SIN taking occasion by the commandment *deceived me* and by it killed me. Therefore the law is holy and just and good. Was that

which is good made death to me?
God forbid. But sin, That it will
appear *sin*, working death in me
by that which is good; that sin by
the commandment might become
exceedingly sinful. (emphasis added)

We can never deny the truth of these
statements, for humankind proves them over
and over. Let us now accelerate the time
machine to the end of this paradise on earth.
About the very end of it, the record prophesies
as follows:

> And when the 1000 years are
> expired, Satan will be let out of his
> prison, and shall go out to deceive
> the nations which are in the four
> quarters of the earth, Gog and
> Magog, to gather them together
> to battle: their number is like the
> sand of the sea. And they went up
> on the breadth of the earth, and
> surrounded the camp of the saints,
> and the beloved city: and fire came
> down from God out of heaven, and
> devoured them.

And the devil that deceived them was cast into the lake of fire and brimstone, where the antichrist and the false prophet *are* and shall be tormented day and night for ever and ever. (emphasis added)

9

The Mystery of Rock and Precious Stones

Rock has been a great treasure for humankind throughout history. It is found on earth in many forms and has many uses. It varies greatly in value. We marvel at the rock-building art of the ancient world. Rock has a great spiritual meaning in the message and function of God's purposeful revelation to us in His Word.

Going back in time to a message from God, we read,

> And all the congregation of the children of Israel journeyed from the wilderness of sin, after the Lord's commandments; and pitched their tents in Rephidim: and there was no water for the people to drink, so they were chiding Moses, demanding water to drink. And Moses said, why ask me? Why do you tempt the Lord? And Moses cried to the Lord, saying, what shall I do for

these people? They are almost ready to stone me. And the Lord said to Moses, gather the elders and take them and your staff with you, and I will stand upon the Rock in Horeb. There you shall strike the rock, and water will flow out of it. So Moses did as the Lord commanded.

We see a great miracle here. First, the Lord is proving His existence by standing on the rock, even though He cannot be seen. It is not possible to strike a solid rock and break it with a wooden stick. The Lord is telling the people, essentially, "I am more powerful than this great immoveable stone. You know now that I am the almighty God, and I am among you: and you know that I give the water of life."

In spiritual truth, God is the one from whom all life flows. This great rock is a symbol used over and over in the Word of God to represent Himself as He deals with His people. In the record, the Lord is recorded to have said to Moses, "You and the people depart from here, and continue toward the land I promised to Abraham, Isaac and Jacob ... and I will send an angel before you, and I will drive out the

Canaanite, the Amorite, the Hittite, Perizzite, and the Hivite, and the Jebusite: till you go into the land flowing with milk and honey. You are a stiff necked people, and I will not go with you, lest I should consume you on the way."

In response, the record tells us,

> And Moses said to the Lord; "See you have said to me, Bring up this people: and you have not let me know whom you will send with me. Yet you have said; I know you by name, and you have found grace in my sight ... please show me your way, that I may know you, find grace in your sight: and consider that this nation is your people." And God said, "My presence will go with you, and I will give you rest" ... And Moses said, "I beseech you *show me your Glory.*" And he said, "I will make all my goodness pass before you, and I will proclaim the name of the Lord before you: and will be gracious to whom I will be gracious, and show mercy to whom I will show mercy. You cannot see my

face: for no man can see it and live.
There is a place by me, and you shall
stand upon that Rock; and while my
glory passes by, I will place you in a
cleft in the rock, and will cover you
with my hand while I pass by: and
I will take away my hand: and you
shall see my back parts; but my face
will not be seen" (emphasis added)

So Moses was given a special blessing of the presence of the Lord. Here is the lesson: God placed Moses upon the *rock* that followed them in the wilderness. Moses asked to *know* who went with them. Centuries later, we have this account in the Word of God: "All our fathers were under the cloud, and all passed through the sea; and all were baptized to Moses in the cloud and in the sea; and all ate the same spiritual meat; and all drank the same spiritual rock that followed them, and that Rock was Christ."

This great wonder, and the *answer to Moses' prayer,* is confirmed by the Word of God, thousands of years later:

And after six days, Jesus took
Peter, James, and John his

brother, and brought them up into a high mountain apart, and was transfigured before them; and his face shown as the sun, and his clothing was white as the light. And there appeared to them Moses and Elijah talking with him. Then Peter said to Jesus; Lord, it is good for us to be here: if you will, let us make here three dwellings, one for each of you. Before he finished speaking, a bright cloud overshadowed them: and a voice from the cloud, which said, "This is my beloved Son, in whom I am well pleased; hear him."

This is the mystery: the rock represents the almighty God *and* the Son of God and Man, who was stricken with the rod of a Roman cross. He was crucified by other human beings (in the wilderness, which is to say, in the world), and He now provides living water (salvation) to all who will drink. This one who was crucified and spent three days of death in the tomb and then rose from the dead is now the Rock of salvation to all who call upon Him. Those who call upon Him in truth become the building stones of His church. In fact, He changed Peter's name to Cephas, which means a little stone. Jesus Himself is the chief cornerstone, foundation, and head (Lord) of His church.

The resurrection of our Lord Jesus Christ was more than two thousand years ago, but there is still the mystery of the *precious stones*: God has shown us many wonderful things of Himself, going back to the time when Israel was finally dwelling in the Promised Land. The Lord issued instructions to the high priest concerning the temple worship:

> You shall take gold, and blue, and purple, and scarlet, and fine woven linen, with cunning work. And you shall make a Vesture for the high priest. It shall have two shoulder pieces, joined at the two edges, with the artistic girdle of it made with the same materials.
>
> You shall take two Onyx Stones; and engrave the names of the children of Israel on them. Six of their names on each one, according to their birth. You shall make them

with settings of gold. You shall put the two stones upon the shoulders of the Vesture for stones of memorial; and Aaron shall wear their names before the Lord. And you shall make the breastplate of judgment with artistic work the same as his Vesture. You shall set in it four rows of stones engraved with the names of the children of Israel in the rows.

The four rows of stones that God requests would look like this:

First:	Reuben	Simeon	Levi
	Sardius	Topaz	Garnet
Second:	Judah	Issachar	Zebulun
	Emerald	Sapphire	Diamond
Third:	Dan	Napthali	Gad
	Jacinth	Agate	Amethist
Fourth:	Asher	Joseph	Benjamin
	Beryl	Onyx	Jasper

See this mystery that unfolds when we look at the meaning of these names again.

Reuben means, "see a son." The firstborn of Jacob and the firstborn of God, Jesus the Christ is also the only begotten Son of God, given to be a sacrifice for our sins. Reuben's stone is Sardius, which is red, the color of the blood of the sacrifice. This is a clear type and picture of the Lord Jesus Christ.

Judah means, "praise." Judah was the fourth son. Emerald green is the color of the rainbow around the throne of God. This speaks of the rainbow of promise that God the Creator made to humankind and of the *Lion of the tribe of Judah.* There will not be another flood to destroy humankind.

Joseph means "adding." Remember that Joseph was the one hated and cast away by his brethren to become the savior of the world. Joseph is a picture and type of the Lord Jesus Christ, who was *added* to humankind by God to be its Savior. This also speaks of the first appearance of the perfect man, the Lamb of God. Onyx is the first of four stones called "most precious," just as the Son of Man is most precious. It is also remarkable to understand that these two stones carry *all* the people of Israel and just one Savior.

Benjamin means "son of my power." This is another picture of Christ the Lord when He returns to earth to rule with all power. Please note the stone is *jasper*. Jasper is *not* a gem quality stone; it is the most abundant colorful stone on earth, in fact. It is as common as common can be. We remember that the Lord Jesus Christ came to earth as the poorest of men: He said, "the Son of man has no place to lay his head." We also should note that the one who sits upon the throne in heaven has the appearance of both the *jasper* and the *sardius*. Benjamin is the son of God's power, like the Son of Man who shed His blood to save humankind. Jasper, a stone for a common man joins with Sardius, God's blood-red stone and the one who followed Israel in the wilderness. This truth of these stones extends throughout eternity, according to the record: "The bride the Lamb's wife ... the great city, the holy Jerusalem, descending out of heaven from God; having the glory of God: and her light was like to a stone *most precious*, even like a *jasper* stone, clear as crystal."

The fourth most precious stone is sapphire, which refers to Issachar, the fifth son of Jacob's wife, Leah. Remember that five is the number of grace, the church dispensation. This dispensation is also spoken of as the church age. Here is the connection: "Then they that feared the Lord spoke often one to another: and the Lord listened, and heard it, and a *book of remembrance* was written before him for them that feared the Lord, and that thought upon his name. And they shall be mine, says the Lord of hosts, in that day when I make up my *jewels*; and I will spare them, as a man that spares his own son that serves him" (emphasis added).

To summarize, we have one and two, Jasper And Sardius, on the Throne with God and the Son of Man. Then we have three, which is onyx, Joseph, and Immanuel (in type), all proclaiming that God is with us. Finally, we have four, which is sapphire, referring to the jewels of the church and to all of God's own of all ages.

We can see the relationship between precious stones and books. Now we will examine the mystery of the books of God.

10

The Mystery of the
Books of God

Why should there be a book of God? Many
have told us about the Book of Books: the Holy
Bible. Within that book there are many others.
They are as follows:

God's Book

The Lord God wrote this book before He
created the universe. He had a perfect plan and
purpose for this book. It is the *birth record of every
human being.* The Lord knew what each one of us
would be like. He foresaw that each one, except
for Jesus, would be a sinner, and that all our
offspring would be sinners in the same way, by
birth and by free choice. Some would be great,
some would be famous, some would be small
and infamous, and some would accomplish great
things and be called great. Some would waste the
precious lives He gave them on the selfish pursuit
of pleasure, a hunger born in every one of us.

That hunger can only be filled by God Himself. In His mercy, he provided for that need, as the eternal record states: "God has chosen us [His own believers] to salvation through sanctification of the Spirit and Belief of the Truth." God does not want anyone to suffer an eternal death. That does *not* prevent us from dying. We also must make a choice to receive Him through belief in His truth. For this reason, He wrote His book of truth so that we would know to make the right choice.

Who is written in God's book? *Everyone.* Yes, that is correct: every human was written there before creation. But remember, *some will be blotted out.* From the words of Moses, a great prophet of God, we read, "And Moses returned to the Lord and said, Oh, this people have sinned a great sin, and have made themselves gods of gold. Yet now, if you are willing, please forgive them; but if not, blot me, I pray thee, out of your book that you have written." And then the Lord said to Moses, "Whoever sins against me, I will *blot out* of my book. Therefore go on now, and lead the people to the place I told you of; behold my angel will go before you; never the less, in the day when I visit, I will visit their sin upon them" (emphasis added).

Well, we might ask, how can we know who will be blotted out? By these words, we know:

> Blessed be the God and Father of our Lord Jesus Christ, who has chosen us in Christ himself; before the foundation of the world, that we should be holy and without blame before him in love; having Predetermined, that we should be adopted children by Jesus Christ to himself, according to the good pleasure of his will. To the praise of the glory of his grace, wherein he has made us accepted in the beloved. In whom we have redemption through his blood, the forgiveness of sins, according to the riches of his grace; wherein he has abounded toward us in all wisdom and understanding; having made known to us the Mystery of His Will, according to his good pleasure which he has purposed in himself.
>
> That in the Administration of the fulness of times, he will gather together in one all things in Christ, both which are in heaven, and which are on earth; even in Him.

So now we know His plan, we must work and study to understand it. The place we will search is in the books of God, *within* the Book of Books.

Book of Covenant and Law

After God delivered Israel from Egypt, the people Israel immediately turned back into the worship of false gods: "With many of Israel, God was not well pleased: for they were overthrown in the wilderness." God now chose to make a sacred agreement with His Israel so that there would be no doubt about the will and purpose of God for His people:

> Israel camped before the mountain in Sinai, and Moses went up to God, and the Lord called to him out of the mountain, saying, You shall tell the house of Jacob, the children of Israel; you have seen what I did to the Egyptians, and how I bare you on eagles wings, and brought you to myself. Now therefore, if you will obey my voice indeed, and keep my covenant, then you shall be a peculiar treasure to me, above all people: for

all the earth is mine. And you shall
be to me a kingdom of priests, and
a holy nation. These are the words
to tell Israel. And Moses told them
these words ... and all the people
said ... "All that the Lord has spoken,
we will do" ... Then Moses took the
Book of the Covenant and read it in the
hearing of the people: and they said:
"All that the Lord has said we will do,
an be obedient." (emphasis added)

Of course we know that Israel could not keep
the Commandments and ordinances of God,
just as we have not been able to do so. It is only
by His grace that we are saved and have become
His children. How can we be sure that when we
have received the Lord Jesus Christ that we can
never be lost again and will have that eternal life
He has promised? We know this from the next
part of the eternal record of humankind.

Book of Life

This is the book containing the names of *all*
of God's redeemed of all time. There can be
no mistake here. The names were already

entered in this book *before* creation began. The eternal record states, "For as much as you know that you were not redeemed with corruptible things, as silver and gold, from your vain conversation received from your fathers; but with the precious blood of Christ, as of a lamb without blemish and without spot: who verily was ordained before the foundation of the world, but was made manifest in these last times for you."

Without question, this plan of redemption existed before creation. But we ask, how can we be sure of our names? We are clearly told in God's eternal Word concerning the unsaved *and* His own children in the days of tribulation, "Those that dwell on the earth will wonder [about the Antichrist] whose names were *not written* in the book of life from the *foundation* of the world" (emphasis added). Further questioning this record, many will ask how we can know our names are there. The apostle Paul, in writing to the Christian assembly located in Philippi, says, "And I entreat you also, true yoke fellow, help those women who labored with me in the gospel, with Clement also, and with others of my fellow laborers, whose names *are in the Book of Life*!" (emphasis added).

Paul knew the people whose names were in the book by the evidence they carried with them. This is wonderful. If we examine these people and people like them in this same letter that Paul wrote to the Philippians, we can learn from their various forms of evidence. *Examining these writings* we find most interesting things. It is possible to read people by observation. As Paul's wrote, "Do we need letters of commendation to you, or letters from you? *You* are our *letter* written in our hearts, *known* and *read* of all men. For as much as you are manifestly declared to be the *letter* of Christ, ministered by us, written not with ink, but with the Spirit of the living God; not in tables of stone, but in the fleshly tables of the heart" (emphasis added). We can read Paul's observations of the people whose names are in the Book of Life. I list them here from his writing:

1. Paul addresses all the saints in Christ Jesus who live in Philippi. Every Christian is *in* Christ: "For by one Spirit

we are all Baptized into one body [the body of Christ]."

2. We are participating in the gospel. (We have believed, received, and obeyed the Word of God with our lives.)

3. God, who has *begun* this good work in us, *will perform it until the day of* Jesus Christ.

4. You are partakers of the same grace that Paul has been given.

5. You are being filled with the *fruits* of righteousness (and the fruits we bear can be read by all).

6. Christians can speak the Word of God without fear.

7. Christ is magnified in our bodies, whether by life or by death.

8. Christians strive for the faith of the gospel.

9. Christians have *conflicts* with the world we must live in.

10. Let this *mind* be in you, which was also in Christ Jesus, who made Himself of no reputation and took on the form of a servant. (In another letter, Paul said, "We have the mind of Christ.")

11. It is God working in you both to will and to do His good pleasure.

12. Be blameless and harmless, children of God; be without rebuke, in the midst of a crooked and perverse nation, among which you shine as lights in the world.

13. *We* hold forth (share), the word of *life*, God's Word.

14. Christians worship God in the Spirit and have *no* confidence in the flesh.

15. We have righteousness, which God gives us by faith.

16. Our citizenship is in heaven, from where we look for the Savior, the Lord Jesus Christ. The record says, "Therefore there is laid up for me a crown of righteousness, which the Lord, the righteous judge, shall give me in that day: and not to me only, but to all those who also love His appearing."

There is more proof as follows: We must grow up into Christ. We must be changed into and conformed to his image. Christ must be formed in us; we must bear the image of the heavenly. We must be partakers of the divine nature. Christians *must* bear fruits of Christ, who is the Vine (we know people by their fruits). These from the Word:

1. Holiness
2. Knowledge of Christ
3. Righteousness (given by God)
4. Thanksgiving to God
5. Soul winning
6. Labor (bearing His yoke)
7. Giving to God's work

Book of the Living

The Book of the Living comprises the names of those who survive and live through the tribulation.

The Opened "Little" Book

The Opened "Little" Book is another name for the book of Revelation.

The Book of Works

The Book of Works cannot save anyone!

11

The New Heaven and the New Earth

The mystery of humankind: should we ever fully come to know it? Everything described in the eternal record is the final answer to all we have questioned in our search for answers. The refusal of human beings to accept the truth and change our lives for our own good appears to be the reason for the final and ultimate climate change. Does logical reason still exist in the minds of human beings? We might wonder about that as we examine this great climate change. The eternal record tell us as follows:

> That you may be mindful of the words which were spoken before by the holy prophets, and of the commandment of us the apostles of the Lord and Savior: knowing this first, that there shall come in the last days scoffers, walking after their own lusts, and saying: Where is the

promise of his coming? For since the fathers fell asleep, all things continue as they were from the beginning of creation.

For this they are willingly ignorant of, that by the word of God the heavens were of old, the earth standing out of the water and in the water: Whereby the world that was then, being overflowed with water perished: But the heavens and the earth that are now, by the same word are kept in store, *reserved* to fire in the day of judgment and eternal damnation of ungodly men. But be not ignorant of the fact that one day is with the Lord as a thousand years, and a thousand years as one day.

The Lord is not slack concerning his promise, as some men count slackness; but is long suffering toward us, not willing that any should perish, but that all should come to repentance. For the day of the Lord shall come as a thief in the night; in which the heaven shall pass away with a great noise, and the elements *will melt with fervent heat,*

> *the* earth *also and the works in it shall be*
> *burned up.* (emphasis added)

Seeing, then, that all of these things will be dissolved, what manner of people should we be in all holy conversation and godliness, looking for the fast coming of the day of God, when the heavens being on fire shall be dissolved, and the elements shall melt with great heat? We, according to His promise, look for a new heaven and a new earth in which righteousness dwells.

Now we know, as the prophet wrote of his time and ours. We also know there must be a great kingdom of the Lord Jesus Christ on this present earth lasting for a thousand years. From this description of earth's final days, we can see the answer to the question of why there will be a *new heaven and a new earth.*

It is amazing that one thing, *sin*, must be eliminated from existence. Even a total healing of our planet and a thousand years of peace and righteous government by the Prince of Peace Himself do not erase sin. But God will not be defeated; wrong of all forms must cease to exist forever. So let us look at this new and wonderful place the Lord has created, as depicted in the eternal record of humankind: "And I saw a new heaven and a new earth: for the first heaven and the first earth are passed away: and there was *no more* sea" (emphasis added). We have heard all our lives (falsely) about how all things, including human beings, came from the sea!

The record continues: "And I saw the holy city, new Jerusalem, coming down from God out of heaven, prepared as a bride adorned for her husband. And I heard a great voice out of heaven saying, behold the dwelling place of God is with men, and he shall dwell with them, and they shall be his people, and God himself shall be with them, and be their God."

Here, then, is the mystery of humankind revealed. There is everlasting life for humankind. God has ordered it and promised it, so nothing and no one can prevent *eternal life with God* except for human beings ourselves. As it is written, "Seeing you [the non-believers] have put [the Word of God] from you, ... that choice judges yourselves Unworthy of everlasting life." The record also says, "The days of our years are three score years and ten years; and if by reason of strength, they be fourscore years, yet is their strength *labor* and *sorrow*; for it is soon cut off, *and we fly away*" (emphasis added). God's eternal Word tells the truth about the people of earth.

The *Final* Mystery

The final mystery has not yet been revealed; that is the mystery of God Himself. But He will reveal it according to His promise, as recorded in the Holy Bible: "And the angel standing upon the sea and upon the earth, lifted up his hand to heaven, and swore by him that lives for ever and ever, and who created heaven and the things therein and the earth and the things that therein are, and the sea and the things which are therein, that there should be time no longer: but in the days of the voice of the seventh angel, when he shall begin to sound, the Mystery [of all mysteries] of God Himself should be finished, as he has declared to his servants the Prophets."

The seventh angel will sound in the tribulation, even while God pours out His judgment on a world that hates Him, and even then, many will reject Him. The record tell us, "But sin that it might appear sin, working death in me by that which is good; that sin by the commandment might become exceeding sinful." Humankind's sin began on earth. Now everything about that sin must be totally erased! Even earth itself.

However, God *wins*! For God so loved the world that He gave His only begotten Son, that whoever believes on Him should not perish, but have everlasting life!

I hope to see you at the greatest event planned for all eternity; the address, according to the eternal record, is as follows: "let us be glad and rejoice, and give honor to him: for the marriage of the lamb is come, and his wife has made herself ready. And to her it was granted that she that should be arrayed in fine linen, clean and white: for the fine linen is the righteousness of saints. And he said to me, write, saying, they are blessed whomever are called to the marriage supper of the lamb. And he said to me, these are the true sayings of God."

The End

Printed in the United States
By Bookmasters